THE BURNHAMS BOOK
OF
CHARACTERS AND MEMORIES

Compiled by Raymond Monbiot

Published in 2002 by:
Rotherfield Management Ltd
Eastgate House
Overy Road
Burnham Market
Norfolk
PE31 8HH

© Raymond Monbiot

ISBN 0 9542567 0 0

Typesetting:
Raymond Monbiot

Printed by:
BARNWELL'S OF AYLSHAM
Penfold Street,
Aylsham, Norfolk
NR11 6ET

Contents
page

Foreword

In 1966 a woman aged 106 recalled the memories her grandfather had recounted to her as a child, of the Battle of Waterloo at which he had fought in 1815. On the morning after the battle, the field was white – the last thing one might have imagined. But white cotton wads of spent cartridges lay thick upon the ground and gave it this mantle.

This kindled my interest in living history. Most of the contributors to this book have lived in the Burnhams all their lives and their memories and stories extend back, in some cases, through seven decades. However these have rarely been committed to paper and there was a danger that they would be lost for ever. So I set out to capture the stories and anecdotes as they were told to me. *The Burnhams Book of Characters and Memories* is the result.

The Burnhams have changed a great deal over the last 30 years. This traditional, labour intensive, agricultural community has given way to the support services of its exploding tourist, holiday and weekend home industry. This is a mixed blessing. The villages were already in a state of decline when that lifeline to the outside world, the railway, contracted in the 1950s and was discontinued altogether in the early 1960s. This closed a chapter for the residents of the Burnhams, many of whom had travelled to school in Fakenham by train from the age of 11, joining it at Heacham, Docking or Burnham Market and changing at Wells next the Sea on the way. It was possible to catch a train from Burnham Market any day of the week, including Sundays, and connect to London in a journey time enviable by today's standards.

Agricultural labour was giving way to machinery and the main purpose of village life was running down. That is until the Burnhams were rediscovered in the 1970s and 1980s in all their beauty and potential, the jewels of North Norfolk.

The pressures on the village to connect with the outside world were well demonstrated in the extreme winter weather of 1979. The roads from the Burnhams had to be dug out of the snow for the villages to function. Yet in 1947 when there was similar isolation, there was no point in digging out a connection with the outside world because the Burnhams were self sufficient.

This opening up of the villages has not been without pain to its residents. Whilst jobs and prosperity have flowed in the wake of the incomers, the pressure on house prices makes it very difficult for local young people to set up home here. The influx of cars is painful in the summer and getting worse most of the year. Yet the influx of visitors and weekenders is essential to the shops and services.

Most visitors are in a hurry to get on with their holidays and do not have the time to look about them at the characters with whom they rub shoulders. The Burnhams are home to academics in arts and sciences, high court judges, fellows of learned societies, retired Air Marshals and Admirals and experts in as wide a range of subjects as will be found in any group of villages. These distinguished residents are as much a part of the scene as the born and bred residents of the villages who have been here for generations, many of whom are just as interesting. There are retired farm workers who have laboured all their lives to feed their families and the nation. They will almost certainly have fought for their country. Their wives and mothers will have struggled to bring up large families without any of the state support that modern families take for granted - and they had to go out to work to make ends meet.

The Burnhams contain a rich mix of characters. Whether they have lived here all their lives or have brought their talent, energy and resources to the benefit of the villages through settling here in retirement, the result is upbeat and vibrant.

Memories can fade after 50 years and events long past may be vested with enchantment or embellishment. Most of the stories in this book are attributable and the characters named. However, a few stories circulate where the characters are not identified. For example the husband who brought some sausages home for his tea and fell asleep. Whilst he slumbered his wife cooked and ate them and smeared his lips with the grease. When he awoke and asked for his tea she told him he had already had it, and licking his lips he was puzzled.

Whilst striving for accuracy I hope my readers will accept that the human memory is fallible. It is all the more interesting for that.

I much appreciate the co-operation and goodwill of those who have made it to these pages. Telling the tale is one thing – seeing it in print is another – and we have worked together on the finished chapters. I am grateful too to our black and white cat, Gabby, who gets me up at crack of dawn each day to get on with the writing.

Raymond Monbiot

Eastgate House
Burnham Market

About the Author

Raymond Monbiot was born in 1937, went to school in London and started work as a trainee with J. Lyons & Co in 1956 humping sacks of flour for the bakery. Trained as a pastry chef, where his duties included making the cakes for Buckingham Palace garden parties, he moved into production management, including foreman on the nightshift, became a van salesman and rose in the ranks to be the National Sales Manager of Lyons Bakery at the age of 24. He managed companies for Lyons until becoming Managing Director of Huntley & Palmers, Jacobs and Peek Frean Biscuits and later Chief Executive of Campbells Soups at Kings Lynn. He is a Liveryman of the Worshipful Company of Butchers, a Freeman of the City of London and, for his political and public services was awarded the MBE in 1981 and the CBE in 1994. He is a columnist and contributor to trade magazines. His first book – *How to Manage Your Boss* – sold 30,000 copies.

In 1961 he married Rosalie Gresham Cooke whose father was a Member of Parliament and whose family has owned the Friary at Blakeney since 1911 – managed today by her brother, the Revd Hereward Cooke, Canon of Norwich Cathedral and a Norwich City Councillor.

Rosalie is Norfolk County Councillor for the Hunstanton Ward, Chairman of the County Council's Social Services Committee and

Chairman of the Board of Visitors of Wayland Prison. She is Chairman of one housing association and a board member of three others. She was awarded the OBE in 1992.

They live in Burnham Market and have two surviving children. George Monbiot is a well known environmental activist, journalist, columnist and author. Eleanor, who lives in Kenya, has extensive responsibilities at World Vision, the second largest humanitarian aid organisation in the world.

Burnham Market

The Baldwins

Gertrude and Fred Baldwin raised eight children – seven boys and one girl. They had moved to Burnham Market from Massingham to find work on the land. Fred was a cowman for the whole of his long career and worked seven days a week without holidays or respite. He lived to be 83 and died in 1977. Gertrude, who was born in Walsingham in 1900, married Fred in 1920 and lived to be 85.

By today's standards the Baldwins are a remarkable family. They had no money other than their wages. Agricultural rates of pay were meagre at the best of times but through recession and change to the employment structure of farming it was harder still. Fred Baldwin earned 37/6d a week for seven days work and gave Gertrude 30/- of it to feed and clothe the family.

He liked a drink but had to earn extra to pay for it. He would sell three or four eggs, which was the price of half a pint of beer, and once in the pub take his chance that he could help anyone who would buy him another. He was a part time barber and itched to get the shears going on a needful head of hair. He would also go round the smallholdings and castrate young animals to earn the extra to have some spending money of his own. He had a rough time in the First World War. He served throughout, taking ammunition in mule drawn carts up to the front line though the mud and the shells. He was a veteran of Ypres and the Somme.

L to R . Stanley, Alan, Sybil, Brian, Ian

Gertrude Baldwin

Stanley Baldwin, the third son and named after the Prime Minister in 1924 when Stanley was born, takes up the story.

"To make ends meet Mother went out to work at Westgate Hall and took in washing at home. As a girl she had worked in a munitions factory in London in the First World War. She handled TNT, which was known to turn the workers' hair yellow and affect their health, usually within a year, but she escaped that fate. In the Second World War years she helped with whist drives and dances in the old red hut which was the village hall at the time, working with Grandma Bee and Mrs Armiger to entertain British and Canadian servicemen from local airfields and the searchlight unit stationed near the village. They used to skate on Stilgoe's pond in winter. She carried on working and was a home help until she was 73.

"There were no family allowances or hand outs from the State.

"The family had to fend for itself and life was hard. We each learned, by the age of 14, to be self sufficient," Sybil remembers. "I worked at the Victoria pub (next to Londis) after school when I was 14, making sandwiches for the Poles and Ukraineans working on the land. I also scrubbed the floors at Mr Guiney's fish and chip shop and café – now Gilly's dress shop. In total I earned 8 shillings per week and was able to buy my first new coat. We expected to make a contribution to the family in chores or wages when we could and did not expect to receive anything we had not earned one way or another.

"My brother Ian worked for Reg Utting four hours a day from the age of 14 and then went on to greater things – scaring crows from daybreak to dark, seven days a week for Case and Stilgoe. He was paid 11/2d a week – the crows never had a day off! Pleasures that we did not make for ourselves did not exist. If it cost money we could not do it.

"We had no shiny new bikes so the older boys would go scavenging for old bike frames, handle bars, wheels and tyres. Then we would fill the tyres with newspaper and there we had a bike for all the family to use.

"The more children one had the harder it was, but large families were quite usual and neighbours helped each other. No one locked their doors, money was left out for the coalman without any concern that it might be stolen and the children played in and out of each others' houses like a big extended family."

The Baldwins lived in a cottage on the Creake Road opposite the present Burnham Motors. "All eight of us plus another who died soon after birth, were born over the span of 15 years," says Sybil. "Each of us had our chores to do and we got on with it. There had to be order in the way the family was run. Father would not stand any nonsense and Mother looked to us all to help her run the house and raise the family. She would wash and feed the youngest and it would then spend the rest of the morning in the pram. A plank was placed across the door of the cottage so the crawlers could not wander off into the interesting world beyond.

"My particular job each day, when I came home from school, was to lift up, shake out and brush the coconut matting in the kitchen area. This was the main walk through and the most used part of the house, attracting crumbs, spillages and the weather on our boots. By the age of 11 I was more or less running the household."

"We had respect for our parents," says Alan. "We never answered them back and realised at a very young age that co-operation from all of us was essential for the family to function. We were always on the look-out for something to ease the pressure. This could be a swede in the road, a rabbit, a piece of abandoned coal or some wood for the fire. The

Wedding Group, Fred & Gertrude on left

line between what was acceptable and what was not was clear. We were a tough family but we knew the line between right and wrong. We respected each other, our parents and our neighbours and we made the most of the strength of family life."

Stanley remembered the early tasks they took on for wages. "We took whatever work was going from an early age. We were all Hold Ye (Holgee) boys during harvest from about the age of eight. When the cattle had been sold at the Market each week from the yard above the Hoste, a gang of boys would drive them to the pens at the railway station to await shipment. A whole day's work driving 15 or so cattle at a time earned us each 1/-. We had an allotment and that fed us our potatoes and vegetables. Most allotment holders kept a pig and in wartime if you killed a pig it meant forgoing six months' meat ration.

"We lived off rabbits and hares mainly. You could sell a rabbit for 3d and a rabbit skin for three ha'pence. The rent for the allotment was about 2/6d a year. We collected rosehips and sold them for syrup and went gleaning in the fields where we sold the recovered corn back to the farmer. Then there was work in the pea harvests where we could earn 1/- a bag pea picking. It was all hand picking and cows were milked by hand. There was no spraying of crops in those days and we could earn 3d per hour pulling out weeds in the corn.

"There were 40 agricultural workers on Case and Stilgoe's 1000 acre Crabbe Hall farm before the war and most of us worked there at one time and another. Those of us who were privileged to work for Jeremy Everitt – the ex champion amateur jockey – at Shammer farm found him to be a fine gentleman and a good friend of the village.

"There were invariably ten of us sitting round the table for meals. At Christmas this increased to 20 and sometimes as many as 30. A rabbit had to go a long way and the members of the family who were working had the best bits. The others had to make do with the offal or the less favoured pieces. Mother would send me shopping into the village with two shillings. With that I bought 3d worth of bones and two pieces of scrag from Barkers the butchers – that is where Howells are today. Then to Searles where I would buy half a pint of split peas and some broken biscuits.

"Most weeks we had 35 loaves of bread delivered by the baker and Mother baked bread on top of that. With the scraps she would make bread and butter pudding or bread pap. We ate porridge and she made real dumplings using suet. We kept a goat or two and the best would give up to 10 pints of milk a day. We had an oil lamp for light and every time the door opened the flame would shoot up and blacken the ceiling. It could also crack the glass which was serious as the replacement cost money we did not have.

"Mother used to cut down clothes to fit us as we grew up. Sometimes this was more successful than others," continued Stanley. "One time I had a pair of trousers where the crotch was below the knees and the waist fitted underneath my arms. I had a strap of material over my shoulders to keep them up. There was a jacket, cut down to size at the pocket with the flap still there but no pocket. The other children at school took it all in their stride, as we did. After all, most of them were poor too, although families with one or two children were better off."

"We could not afford to see a doctor," adds Sybil, who went on to train as a nurse and devoted 33 years to the profession, mainly at Wells Cottage Hospital and then 12 years in the community. She was also a Marie Curie nurse. " We would be given cow remedies which Father used in his work with the cattle. This included black or red medicine for colic. If we cut ourselves the remedy was pepper put straight onto the wound, which stung no worse than iodine. And if we had a skin rash the remedy was cowline! It seemed to work well enough. We were all healthy as we grew up and members of the family generally live to a good age. Operations for such conditions as tonsilitis were performed mainly at home. Nurse Rowland was the midwife who attended most births in the area. She was the wife of the antique dealer in Front Street who numbered Queen Mary among his clientele."

"We were a musical family – at least most of us were," says Alan looking meaningfully at Brian whose talents are many but music is not one of them. "The family swelled the choir at Sunday school where each of us was paid 1/- for our trouble. The vicar appreciated seeing his choir stalls full even if the sound left something to be desired. Mother played the harmonica and could sing like an angel." Alan has an electric organ at home and sings and plays at village functions. He has inherited his mother's talent. "Ian could play the piano although he never had lessons and he could dance like a dream," says Sybil. "It was ballroom dancing at the time.

"When we were re-housed into a large four-bedroom council house just before the war the boys would bring friends home. Our next door

Norman and Sybil

neighbour Mr Gorrod had an old shed in his garden and we danced to a wind-up record player. At the time Victor Sylvester was the fashion. Norman was a great ballroom dancer and taught me to dance at the age of 10. Among the local boys who came and danced with us were Billy Bickell, Ken Francis, Dennis Codman and Jack Pearce who still walks his dog in the village. The late Billy Bickell was a particular friend of our third youngest brother Leslie who died years ago. Billy would fight Leslie's battles for him. Another good friend was Eric Skeet who still lives in the village. At night we all had home-made pickled onions and cocoa made with milk."

As the members of the family left school they tended to stay close to home although Norman, the eldest, went to Crawley in Sussex and Lennie went to Leeds, but returned to work in Burnham.

Both Norman and Lennie were Holgee boys from the age of 11 or 12 working seven days a week at harvest time to earn money to pay for their winter boots. When they left school at 14 they worked with their father as stockmen and this went on until they joined the forces . Later Lennie kept pigs on what is now the caravan site at the back of Burnham Motors. Alan went to Lynn Tech, learned to be a welder and brick layer and entered the building trade. Eventually he set up his own building business. He worked for a while at Roy's Nurseries near the present Londis shop. Sybil adds "My brother Ian worked there for many years and it was a big scale business. In the summer we would pick two tons of tomatoes a week from the greenhouses and in the winter we would bunch huge chrysanthemums."

By the time the war broke out Norman and Lennie were of an age to join up and went into the army. Stanley enlisted when he was old enough and spent three years in the Royal Navy. After the war he became a stockman. He slept out for 31 nights as a shepherd one time and earned just £1 for the whole period. Brian worked on farms until he chose to become self employed in 1964. "There is plenty of work around if you look for it," he says. " If you do a good job you get recommended from one to another." He cuts hedges, tops meadows, fetches and carries crops and materials and has

Brian

built a strong reputation for his skill, reliability and hard work. At one time he kept 20 sows and a boar and grew loads of vegetables on his allotments.

The Baldwins recall some notable characters in the Burnhams over the years. "Miss de Crepney lived at Norton and went everywhere including to Hunstanton on her two legs. Then there was Mrs Betts who cruised around the village on roller skates when she was not riding her horse – an enormous animal somewhere between a shire and a cart horse that clip clopped through the village at 6 a.m. every day. She would deliver leaflets and letters for certain organisations in which she was interested and was a very well known character.

"The night cart was even better known and to be avoided. Residents of Front Street had no rear access and the nightsoil had to be brought through the house and collected each day by the nightcart. There were usually two men working it and they would stop to buy their lunch at one of the two fish and chip shops in Overy Road. They would park the cart outside and sit on the wall eating. In those days they were making for the Lime Kiln on the Overy Road.

"There were street traders too, selling fish and sea food from Wells. Mr Frairie brought cockles in a cart attached to his bike. Tiny Willis used to tour the village shouting "Fish Alive Alive O!" Then there was Mr Franklin who brought paraffin by cart from North Creake and was known as Mr Sunlight.

"Another character was Jock Monro who lived in Gents Cottage and was a road mender with his own patch to look after. He fascinated us as children because he would walk up and down with his dinner on his head. He wore no shoes claiming that nothing other than the Lord above could hurt him. Cuckoo Moorehouse could imitate any bird, and his brother Tally never did anything. The village barber was Billy Mews, a huge man who puffed a lot. He was likely to disappear in the middle of a haircut to finish his pint in the pub and return to finish the haircut. And George Trett the Baker, whose two horses were lodged in Cooks Meadow, was reputed to be able to sink a good few pints a day and was something of a hero as a result.

"One of the unsung heroes of the village is John Utting. He had to sort out Harold Moorhouse's estate and set up a Trust for the benefit of the villagers who need help in hardship. Also each pensioner receives £50 a year from the Trust and this has been a great contribution from a very public spirited man."

The Baldwins have viewed the development of Burnham Market with mixed feelings. On the one hand the influx of visitors and weekenders has been a great help to the builders and tradesmen. There are 14 builders in the village and standards are generally high. This has brought work and encouraged skills to keep pace with the expansion.

However, as Alan observes, "There are few houses within reach of local families. A farm worker's take home pay today is about £130 a week and he needs to find a house at about £50 or £60 outlay a week to make ends meet. There are very few in that bracket any more. The sale of council houses made the situation worse. The younger generation has to move away from the village and where they have to leave their elderly relatives behind this causes other pressures in their families."

Sybil sees this at first hand. "Since I retired at 62, having gone back to school at 59 to gain the necessary qualifications (trained in nursing skills), I have been looking after the elderly and I now keep house for two of them. One is 92. I also cook for the elderly, sew and make a lot of cakes. After all I have had a lot of experience since the age of 11! One regret I have is that I would like to have gone abroad to, say, Australia or New Zealand as a nurse companion for people who needed care – taking my husband with me!"

The Mannings

The eight Manning children's father William was born in Kings Lynn in 1903, where his father was a carpenter and wheelwright journeyman for Savages, the makers of fairground equipment. William Manning worked wherever he could find it and that was far from easy in the 1920s. Nevertheless he was never out of work and his search took him to London and to a job as clerk in a distribution company.

"His beautiful copper plate handwriting was used as an example to the other clerks with the comment 'this is a man from the turnip fields of Norfolk who is showing you how to write'" says David, his eldest son. Later when he returned to Langham from London, looking for work again in the worst of the Depression, he refused to take a job in the stone pit which was all that was available for young men at the time. So he walked to Yorkshire, sleeping in straw stacks on the way, and eventually found work in Derbyshire as a cowman. He returned again to Langham, Norfolk and met Bertha Coppin who had been born in Burnham Market and who was head cook at Langham Hall. They married in 1930. They went to live in Langham where William found work at Crafers farm. One of his brothers is still alive and lives in Canada at the age of 100.

Trevor and David Manning

David was born in 1933. "We lived in my early days in a cottage adjoining the church on the Field Dalling Road. When the war came the RAF took over Langham aerodrome and blast walls were built outside the cottage to protect it from enemy action. Three weeks after it was completed we were given a fortnight to get out as it had been decided to demolish the building to make an entrance for an army camp.

"We moved from the cottage in the Field Dalling Road to Hindringham. My father was too old to go to war just as he had been too young to fight in the First World War. He joined the Home Guard and also delivered Sunday papers. There was one influential ex officer living in Stiffkey who took the *Sunday Times*. He insisted that it was delivered to him each week so my father had to be excused Home Guard parade on a Sunday morning to carry out his wishes. We used to bike on the aerodrome and ride at speed under the wings of parked aircraft.

"There were five children in the family by this time. My eldest sister June, who now lives in Docking, started her working life with my sister Janet at Alan Bell's spectacle factory which is now the Catholic church in Burnham Market. Janet was the next born after me and she is married to an American airman. They have three children and live in Atlanta, Georgia. The fourth child was my brother Terry who delighted in pranks and was often on the edge of other people's tolerance. After we moved to Burnham one of his pranks was to crawl into the culvert which carries the Goosebec under Harry Farrow's fish and chip shop and shout to Harry's customers. The effect was startling and caused mild panic. No one was surprised when they found out who was doing it. He has three children, lives in Costessey and runs his own grain handling and farm building business.

"My brother Vardon, who was born in 1941, wanted to be a prison warder but had to work on the farm (which he hated) then worked in insurance and finally became a property developer in Australia. He has now retired back to England and is living near Norwich. He has three children.

"As a family we were very poor and had nothing. However, we never owed money. We were taught that we had to work for everything we wanted and were expected to contribute to the household from an early age. I started work at the age of nine on Saturday mornings when my job was to harness up the horse to a tumbril and fetch two loads of food for the livestock at Cargill farm, Hindringham. This earned me 2/1d. Children in farming communities were issued with blue cards during the war which provided for us to spend 20 half days, or 10 whole days as I contrived to make it, per term on farm work.

"I suppose, educationally I was born at the wrong time. It was an age when rural Norfolk was designated an area of Low Parental Expectation and education included a day a week knitting balaclavas for the troops or assembling gas masks. I attended Langham school and we lived at

Hindringham for four years. There were Italian prisoners of war at Cargill farm. They were easy to get along with and I worked with them putting up wire fences to keep the cattle in.

"My age group was the first to have to stay on at school until 15. My friends had left at 14 and I regretted having to stay an extra year. We used Cook's Meadow as our sports field and I had to pull my future brother in law, Henry Shearing, from under the ice on the pond on one occasion and saved his life in the process. Henry became a cowman at Crow Hall farm. Whilst still at school I did a delivery round for Dudley Bower, the high class grocer in Burnham Market, now Bedfords Estate Agents. The loads we had to lift were staggering by today's standards. We would carry 2 cwt bags of sugar into the shop. That is 224 lb. Today the heaviest unit a worker is required to carry is 56 lb. Farm workers had to carry sacks of grain weighing up to 250 lb up the steps to the granary. Health and Safety would have something to say about it today.

"When I left school in 1948 my first job was working on the land for the Roy family at Crow Hall. When I was 18 I was called up for National Service in the RAF. I enjoyed it but it was a waste of time. I was stationed in Manchester and Ipswich. When I returned I went to work on one of the Roys' farms. The Roy family had extensive farming land in the Burnhams and later divided into three separate family owned businesses which included horticulture and milling besides farming. Philip Roy lived at Cobham House, Sydney was at Overy Mill and Gladstone at Sutton House. Timmy Roy's father Dick owned a nursery where the Mill Green houses have since been built and customers would queue up to buy his tomatoes, cucumbers and great ball chrysanthemums. Timmy has glass houses just outside the village on the Overy Road.

"Whilst farms were run separately, at harvest time all the workers on the Roy farms joined forces to get the harvest in for a contract price. For example we would be paid £38 for the work which could last for three weeks. Normal farm working hours were 7 a.m. to 4 p.m. but at harvest time if the weather permitted we would work until dark. There was a lot of walking continually collecting the sheaves to make them into stooks. It is estimated that we walked some 14/15 miles a day at harvest time. The big privilege was to ride on the tractor drawn binder.

"Every Monday there was a livestock market in the Hoste Yard, and on the way to school I would deliver the rabbits we had bred and return for the money on the way home. A rabbit would fetch 1/9d and a good one 2/-. While working for the Roys I would drive two or three days old bull calves to the market, and from the farm we would drive the bullocks to the station. There were geese and ducks for sale and old fashioned horse floats transported much of the livestock. There was also a Monday auction market on the Green in front of Westgate Church which continues to this day.

"For the last 10 years of my working life I was a gardener in North Creake, firstly to the Earl of Dumfries – a noted racing driver who came to the area to understudy Nigel Mansell – and then to John Phelps whose family lived at Bayfield Hall near Holt. I played cricket for Burnham Market for years and, in the days when farms employed large numbers of workers, I played for the farm team competing in the farmers' cricket league against other farm teams.

"At the end of the war we moved to Crow Hall Farm on the Docking Road about two miles from Burnham Market, where Trevor was born in 1946 and Alexandra and Colleen were to follow."

Trevor Manning takes up the story.

"When I was five years old my mother announced that I was going to school. She put me on the bus on the first morning of term to the old school where Olivers Lighting now is. I was there until we were all moved to the new school site in Friars Lane. We would queue in the street for our school dinners, waiting to be served in the building where Natwest bank now is and where Mrs Annie Franklin was head cook. It was good solid plum duff food and not at all bad. The Headmaster at the time was Albert Evans who always appeared to be

Trevor Manning

in awe of his wife. Boys and girls were educated separately. My favourite subject was carpentry and I was good at it. We were taught by Mr Clarke and carpentry lessons continued at the old school site after the rest of the school had moved to Friars Lane. It was my best subject by far.

" I always had the impression that the school was not serious about giving me, and a number of my contemporaries, an education. We seemed to spend a lot of time gardening around the new school, which had to provide vegetables for school meals, rather than learning more brain demanding subjects. As a result some left school unable to read or write with any fluency. This was the fault of the system at the time.

"One of our teachers was Harry Duckworth. He was very religious and played the ukelele. Going to carpentry and science classes at the old school might have been seen as an opportunity to miss assembly but there was no escape and he would wait for us in the street with his ukelele and expect us to join in hymn singing. When the school moved to Friars Lane we still had to go into the village for a haircut. To do this in the lunch hours, having eaten the school dinner, and be back in time for lessons in the afternoon was a scramble. It was not made any easier when the barber, Billy Mews, tended to wander off to a cupboard to drink beer from a jug and the rest of the haircut was completed to heavy breathing and alcohol fumes. We sat with one side of our heads in the light so it was difficult for him to compare each side of the head to ensure an even cut .

"I was the only one in the family who wanted to go into farming , but never did. My father took the view that enough of the family were employed in agriculture and as the youngest son it was not an option for me. However I had been doing Saturday morning work on the farm since I was 10 years old and driving a tractor during the beet season. The other farm workers put sixpence in the hat for my wages when I did so. My first harvest was at the age of 12 when I had to pretend I was 13 to ride on the back of the baler for the Roys. Gladstone Roy would never commit himself as to whether I had a job or not. He would say 'We'll see my man' and the first I knew I had a job was the first morning of harvest when 'Gladdie' said 'If you don't jump on, my man, he'll go without you.' Schoolboys who worked on the farm during harvest were allowed to extend the school summer holiday until harvest was complete. (I longed for a prolonged, wet harvest as I hated school.)

"When I left school I was apprenticed to Alan Pentney, carpenter for Robert Powell, builder of South Creake. I borrowed Vardon's bike to attend the interview. It was an example of how little we travelled from our own village that when I reached North Creake I had to ask the way to South Creake. At the end of my apprenticeship I stayed on with Robert Powell until he retired. I was then 26 and decided to launch out on my own. This was in 1972. I contacted our regular customers and asked them to give me a chance. It was slow going for the first two or three years but as I branched out into general building work it started to grow. I decided to push it harder in the early 1980s and have built it to a size where I can continue to give personal service to our loyal regular customers, many of whose fathers were customers in the past.

"I have deliberately kept the business the size it is with six people working as well as my wife Anne, who does much of the administration, and me. These include my son Mark and my son in law Neil. We have four children and six grandchildren."

"The villagers used to communicate better with each other years ago," adds David. "There was a meeting point at Shrubbery wall, Creake Road, where up to 15 lads would meet in the inlet to the iron gate opposite the playing field. There was little traffic to shoot round the corner to endanger life and interrupt our chatter. There were other gathering points in the village at a time when there was no television to watch and people sought out each other's company. Mike Paget, the gamekeeper, was among those who would spend hours in the road chatting about this and that. Socials were held in the village hall run by the local Labour Party and Billy Ives provided the music.

"There were characters to talk about. Reggie Barwick, known as Shaky, would cure his bacon on a chain hanging down the inside of his chimney. Jimmy Petchey was gardener to Gladdie Roy at Sutton House and was instructed to pick the pears. 'But I have no ladder and can't reach them,' Jimmy said. Gladdie, who was a bit of a comedian, said in jest 'in that case you'll have to cut the tree down.' When Gladdie returned home he couldn't get in because Jimmy had felled the pear tree right across the drive way. Jimmy was famed for singing *Oh for the Wings of a Dove* at the top of his voice.

"There was one husband who would tell his wife he was going to the pub for a few minutes as she prepared Sunday lunch. He would stay there for hours. She would get fed up and on one occasion, put his meal on a tray and slammed it down in front of him at the bar. He complained that she had forgotten the salt and pepper.

"The village has lost much of its earlier atmosphere as local people moved out, the agricultural demand for labour declined drastically, the motor car invaded and weekenders and newcomers have moved in. However, it has also lost the poverty and dereliction which were features of times past. There was real hardship when, the larger the family, the poorer it was, with no state aid or family allowances. The village found a new lease of life when it was 'discovered' in the 1970s. But with mutual respect we live well enough together."

The Stimpsons

From 1906 to 1976 the Stimpson family were the post masters of Burnham Market. Frederick Stimpson, a farrier by profession, came from Burnham Thorpe and had many generations of family ties to the Holkham Estate. He moved to Burnham Market and a change of career. "Perhaps he foresaw the demise of the horse as motor transport and traction grew," says Roy Stimpson, his grandson, who lives in the house just behind the post office in Burnham Market where Vincent Sandall the saddler lived in those earlier days. "The motor car and the tractor were starting to make an impact in the early 1900s and a new era of transport and farm power was about to begin."

Cindy & Roy Stimpson

The post office and the mail service were the only means of communication to and from the world outside the village for most people in the early 1900s. There were few telephones and of course none of the other means of communication we take for granted today. Four postmen were employed by the post office to cover Burnham Market and the villages around twice a day – often picking up outgoing mail for their customers. They also delivered post on Christmas Day.

The post office itself was a going concern without having to expand its range of goods as most do today, although it did sell sweets. Older customers recall its distinctive aroma – a combination of mail bags, sealing wax, brown paper and string. The post master used the sealing wax on registered mail. He would put a flame to the orange/red sealing wax

23

stick and drip and spread the hot wax over parts of the string and on to the brown paper. Then he would apply the crown seal. Roy Stimpson recalls two long counters in the shop.

"My grandfather would open up the shop at 6 a.m. to receive the incoming mail from Kings Lynn. The delivery van would have dropped off the relevant mail bags at other villages on the way and picked up the outgoing mail. The mail bags were sealed with a lead tag. This would be removed at the post office, and sometimes as children, to our delight, we were allowed to remove it under supervision. The contents were shot out onto one of the two long counters in the shop. The mail had been random bundled for Burnham Market at Kings Lynn and tied with string.

"The bundles were then opened up and letters reallocated to the four post delivery rounds. Then the postman for each round would sort the mail into delivery order and set off on a bike in all weathers with parcels in the tray at the front, repeating the process for the second post in the afternoon. Four of the postmen I can remember were Reggie Baldry, Vincent Sandall, Mrs Sandall who took on the Sutton Estate round, and Cyril Woodhouse. In the post office there were displayed on the wall my grandfather's certificate as a qualifying farrier, the horseshoes he had made to obtain his certificate and the portrait of his donkey. I still have the portrait and the certificate and the horseshoes now belong to my daughters – his great granddaughters.

"Christmas time was the peak of the year for letters, parcels and activity. The whole family lent a hand and sausage rolls and mince pies were laid on for all who helped. When Cindy and I married 30 years ago, and my father and mother kept the post office, this became one of her jobs. It was a demanding job to keep up with the appetites of the workers. The yard at the side of the post office was full of parcels, delivered by a three-ton Ford van from Kings Lynn. In those days Christmas cards were less the fashion. Those living in the village would be unlikely to send cards to each other but it was a way of communicating further afield to and from those one did not see every day.

"These were the days when groups of people would gather at Stilgoe's corner or outside the post office or at the village pump near Snellings' butchers shop at the corner of Herrings Lane, to exchange news and chat. Many of them would have started work at 7 a.m. and been on their own all day, not hearing a human voice until they got together in the evening after work. People in those days sought out each other's company. A sight I remember was the rows of radio accumulators re-charging on the long table of Alan Utting's shop. Each weekend these would be brought in to be charged, from all around the district, and a re-charged one picked up. How he or anyone else knew which one belonged to whom was a mystery.

"My grandfather was a well respected man in the village. He knew everyone and his post office was a central part of life. In World War II he was appointed Quartermaster to the Home Guard and was responsible for the arsenal. After the war there was a remaining stock of 12 bore cartridges and we discovered they had a single solid ball in place of the shot. What damage this would have done to the shotgun and the person firing it in the event of an invasion we could only speculate. It would have been a deadly weapon to fire at the enemy at least once! Shotguns were widely possessed in the countryside and their use with appropriate ammunition was logical in time of war. Dad's army would have been in the front line had we been invaded. Preparations were a serious business.

"My grandfather was capable of some subtle subterfuge which would have been invaluable in action. During an exercise his platoon had to mount an attack on HQ which was at R. D. Hancock's house in Burnham Norton. Entry was difficult, of course, so my grandfather got on his bike with his telegram pouch strapped to his back and claimed he had a telegram for urgent delivery for Hancock. He was waved through the sentries and walked into the lounge where he placed a box on the table announcing that it was a bomb and they were all dead.

"He was involved in most village activities. He played the violin and the piano in the village band which was much in demand for ballroom dances and other social events. He was Secretary of the Flower Show for many years.

"My father was born in 1909 and took over as post master on my grandfather's death in 1954. In fact it was my mother who did most of the work of post master while my father was involved with other jobs and activities. He was a man of many parts. He left for the USA at the age of 17 to join an uncle who was a chauffeur. My father's first job was also as a chauffeur and gentleman's gentleman to a millionaire from Kentucky. The latter had a string of racehorses and his racing colours were black and white. When he held a dinner party during the racing season all the decor was black and white. He returned to Burnham Market in the late 1930s when my grandmother died .

"He did work as a mental nurse and was a driver for a while for Silcock's animal feeds of Aylsham where he met and married my mother. During the war he was in the RAMC, as a mental nurse, and spent much of his time looking after shell shocked wounded. He would transport them to a hospital ship off the Gambia during the North African campaigns. He obviously had some sad and harrowing experiences which he would not discuss after he was demobilised at Klagenfurt in 1945. One incident he did recall, however, was a patient determined to leave an aircraft in flight and no amount of persuasion, even striking his hand repeatedly with the buckle of a parachute harness, would alter that intention. In the end my father managed to pull him away – if the door had opened both would have been sucked out to their deaths.

"After the war he again took a series of jobs. One of these was running a mushroom farm for Dr Woodsend who lived at Brancaster. When he took over the post office he was nominally the post master. He had had the good sense to marry my mother who had worked in the post office at Aylsham and she was very capable of taking on the job at Burnham Market. She would open the post office in the morning and my father did one of the rounds. At 12 noon he would relieve her in the shop while she went to cook lunch, returning in the afternoon until 4.30-5.00 when he relieved her again as she went home to prepare tea for the family.

"My father always kept animals. He grazed his horses in the 1970s on Cooks Meadow and kept pigs, cows and calves behind the post office. They ran the post office for 22 years and retired in 1976. My father died in 2000 and my mother lives in Crofts Close."

Roy Stimpson was born in 1943 and the first family holiday he could remember was a week in Bournemouth in 1956. "We did not go on holidays much in those days and certainly not the foreign holidays that so many children expect today. I had an enjoyable childhood with a freedom children do not have today. My father was strict and forthright. If he said snow was black it was black – like his father before him. However, I could roam the countryside aged seven or eight and maybe be out all day dabbling down by the River Burn or in other favourite spots. That would not be possible today where children face more dangers from traffic and worse.

"Mr Evans was headmaster of Burnham School during my time there. I passed the 11+ and went on to Fakenham Grammar School. I was an average student passing five GCEs. I played football but not cricket. I spent a lot of time with my father on Overy beach. The Oppenheim family had a converted Thames barge moored on Scolt Head Point. It had been converted to a three bedroom house boat with two bunks in each bedroom, a kitchen with a gas cooker and all the facilities. They hired it out when they were not using it – which was most of the time. We hired it initially for a week's holiday and my father became its custodian on behalf of the owners. We used to go there on Friday nights after school and my parents would join us around their duties at the post office on Saturdays and for the rest of the weekend. One of the characters at Burnham Overy Staithe was Miss Sheila Disney who wore a navy blue pleated gym slip and had brown legs.

"When I left school I wanted to go farming and my father insisted that we do it properly. This meant time at an agricultural college. So as a first stage I enrolled at Shotesham, south of Norwich, as a student for a one year course. Part way through I received a telegram from my father instructing me to be on the train leaving Norwich at 1.30 on the next Saturday and he would meet me at Wells. There was no explanation and it could have been a family crisis for all I knew. When he met me at the station he told me that John Howard, farmer at Burnham Thorpe, had lost his pigman – killed by a boar – and that I was to take over the job. This was typical of my father. My career had changed even before it had properly begun.

"I was not particularly struck by the college and this was an interesting time in the evolution of the pig industry. John Howard – always a pioneer – was working with Walls to produce a heavy hog. This would produce four ham shoulder joints rather than the traditional two. People wanted ham and Lord Trenchard, the Chairman of Walls Bacon, was driving this innovation hard.

"Before long I became John Howard's assistant and farm secretary. The pig unit moved on and the next venture was prepack vegetables where I became foreman and overseer of 60 women at Whitehouse Farm. One of the products we packed was Victory carrots with Lord Nelson's birthplace on the wrapper. These were sold through distributors based in Yarmouth who were importers of Dutch produce. After two years the supermarket customer decided to change the label to its own brand. Then we ventured into boil-in-the-bag which required considerable capital investment and did not prosper. I moved on to a vegetable prepack co-operative in Suffolk but found the word co-operative inappropriate. It was so frustrating trying to get agreement on anything."

Cindy Stimpson, Roy's wife of 30 years, takes up the story. "We were engaged at the time and I had just started to house hunt. But my prospective father in law was worried about Roy becoming stuck with this co-operative and decided he must come out of Suffolk. True to form he summoned me without explanation to be ready at 6.25 p.m. that evening and he would pick me up by car. I explained that I did not get home from work until 6.00 p.m. but he said 25 minutes to get ready and have my tea was long enough and I must be ready at precisely 6.25 p.m. The object of the trip turned out to be to meet Roy who had been summoned to Attleborough and for me to persuade him to come home. This he did and became production manager at North Creake Produce Packers situated in South Creake where Gilchrist Chocolates are now."

Roy continues, " I was there for three or four years until Tom Wright the manager's sons started to come into the business. I saw an advertisement for a farm secretary for Raynham Farm Co. and was successful in being appointed to the job which I have held now for 30 years. The 6000 acre estate grows contract peas and broad beans as well as other arable crops and has an extensive managed shoot."

Roy as the third generation is proud of the contribution made by his father and grandfather to the village. "They would be a hard act to follow and I have always felt it wise not to compete with their memory."

Cindy, who is one of the Friends of St Mary's Church, was for 12 years a school governor at Burnham and then for seven years at Wells. She is a pianist and organist. "When our two girls were small I was active in the mothers and toddlers group and a playgroup leader. We were both on the PTA and I was also involved as a dinner lady for many years. I really enjoyed contact with the children and see many of them now grown up and developing their talents."

The Stimpson family has served the Burnhams for the best part of a century. Roy and Cindy's daughter Caroline aged 25 works at Bedford Estate Agents while Clare aged 23 works on an alternative therapies website.

Bridget Everitt

The Everitt family connections with the Burnhams go back for generations and the family historian and raconteur – Bridget Everitt – now in her late 70s recalls:

"My great grandfather farmed 1000 acres at Shammer and worked the Maltings, Staithe Street, Wells, where he developed an import export corn business. He also built the school at Creake. He had 16 children and was himself one of 16. Despite this large family most of them were girls and only four married, so today the number of Everitts still in the locality has dwindled.

"One of my great grandfather's 16 children was Thomas, the grandfather of Jeremy Everitt who still lives and farms at Shammer. He lives alone in this enormous house – extended to accommodate a household of 16 children. My great grandfather retired about 1860 and his son, my grandfather, died of throat cancer at the age of 60 in the 1890s. He had eight children, one of whom died as a baby. Two of them became Victorian unmarried ladies typical of their time. They were taught to play

Everitt's Mill

29

the piano, sew a straight line and do charitable works. This lifestyle often turned in on itself and they did little to stimulate their brains. They tended to look after each other and develop quarrelsome behaviour which ended not infrequently, in those restricted days for women, in being 'put away' in their closing years.

"The Victorian unmarried ladies tended to relate with others of a similar mind set. Many of them had little money. They tended to be dogmatic and lonely and expected everyone else to wait upon them. In many ways this made for a sad life and as they got older it led to some eccentric behaviour. The Misses Cook of Eastgate House lived to be 96 and 99 respectively and seldom if ever left the Burnhams in that long life. They were respected by the recipients of their charitable interests and there are numerous stories of their kindness to young or disabled people who looked up to these diminutive and somewhat imperious ladies.

"They held children's parties, usually in fancy dress, which I hated, and avoided if I possibly could. I can remember at the age of five being delivered to such a party, dressed as a fairy. In my embarrassment and rebellion I promptly went into hiding until it was over. I hated having to participate in what I regarded as false fun and resisted my parents' judgement that I was being antisocial. Eventually I went on strike and refused to go to any more of these painful events.

"The two Misses Cook, Miss Maggie and Miss Julia, were diminutive figures. They would be driven around the village in a gig and their driver would refresh himself at the Hoste Arms whilst they were shopping. On Confirmation, they would give the children a prayer book. They were generous to the Guides and Scouts, making a room available for them at Eastgate House where they lived for over 60 years.

" Their fields known as Cook's Meadow, which they let out for grazing horses, were also used for fetes and sports for schoolchildren. At Easter the young of the village would take part in an Easter egg hunt in their grounds. Julia Cook, who was short, slim and wittery, had the most enormous pekinese dog called Teddy which spent its latter years in a bicycle basket and was never required to walk. Maggie Cook had a Cairn terrier which bit everyone.

"One of the most memorable characters in the village and to some, one of the most terrifying, was Carrie Wood, the Burnhams' midwife/nurse. She travelled around on an enormous tricycle which must have weighed a ton. I can see her now riding over the Causeway to Everitt's Mill and down the magnificent avenue of willows and alders which was destroyed in the 1953 floods and has never been replaced. She would arrive for a birth in her large velour hat with her leather bag and stride to the door. She would brook no nonsense or delay. 'Come along, let us get it out of there.' She had the reputation of frightening babies out of their mothers. Carrie lived in a cottage at the gates of Westgate Hall. Whilst many were terrified of her I had a great admiration for her and we got on well. She died aged 80 in the 1950s. Her father was the Rector of Morston and her sister had been married off at the age of 17 to an eccentric middle aged Wells man. They lived in Wells.

" The row of cottages in North Street, oppposite the pink bank cottages, was known as Murderer's Row or Poisoner's Piece after the murders of 1830s. The trial of the two accused was reported at length in *The Times*. The cottages were hard to let because they were rumoured to be haunted still by these events. They have now been converted to part of a private house.

"We had to make our own entertainments in the days before television. The presence of the railway helped a good deal and the trains to Wells and Fakenham, to Hunstanton and Kings Lynn were full both ways. For the adult there were smoking clubs and the Revd Faulkner's newsletters contained full accounts of their excursions. He was the leader of the Band of Hope and if one could prove that no alcohol had passed the lips for a year their reward was tobacco. There were whist drives and a strong Mothers' Union and Womens' Institute. The annual carnival was the big event for the village and attracted crowds from the Burnhams. There was a rousing town band and everyone made and put on fancy dress. The flower and vegetable show was on a grand scale and successful in those days and was accompanied by sports for the children and the adults. All the shops in the village were decorated. It was a major village effort and commitment.

"The main occupation around the Burnhams was farm labouring. At our farm the wages were 30/- a week plus enough land for an allotment at a rent of 2/6 per annum. Most allotment holders had a pig, and bacon and ham hung from kitchen rafters. My father, who had 50 acres and bred Suffolk Punch horses, employed a miller called Sam Bush. When he left to take a job at a mill on the Norwich road he was paid double the salary but none of the perks. He said he always regretted the move because he was worse off. At Harvest Home we held a big party at the farm for all the workers. It went on for two days and it took another two days to get over the quantities of beer and food consumed.

"Utting's ironmongers shop was situated where Fishes is now and it was the most remarkable shop. It always had what you wanted no matter how obscure the request. I can remember being one curtain hook short and debated whether I could go to Uttings and ask for just one hook. After a rummage in the back of the shop a single hook was produced in an envelope. Outside the shop was the area known as the Shambles. There was the wooden photographic studio, Snellings' butchers shop and in the 18th and 19th centuries a lock up jail. Snellings' abattoir was in Aviary Yard, then known as Carpenter's Yard.

"When Mrs Buxton, a grand lady who looked and dressed like Queen Mary, bought The Limes, now Market House, she decided to buy Snellings' butchers shop with the sole purpose of closing it down. She did not regard it as appropriate to the front of her dwelling nor did she appreciate the Salvation Army band and the crowds it brought every Sunday. The lime trees were felled to the shock of the village by a later owner.

"My father was 54 and my mother 44 when I was born. They had one other child, my brother, who was 14 years older than me. At the age of 17 I was 'shot off' to London to learn to live in the big world. I had always wanted to be an actress and my father took a very dim view of such a vulgar occupation for his daughter. He expected me to stay at home and look after my ageing parents. However, my mother had other ideas, being remarkably progressive for her time. So in 1942 I went to London in the middle of the blitz and took digs in Earls Court.

"I enrolled at the Central School of Drama and was there for two years until I was called up.

"I wanted to go into the Wrens but they were full up so I was given three choices: the police – but I was too short – the prison service or a factory. I opted for the factory job. Boring and repetitive as it was, at least I could keep my digs in Earls Court. At the end of the War I went back to drama. Then I joined a rep company and played Yarmouth and Gorleston. Later I was in Reading and Camborne in Cornwall. They were great companies and I loved it, playing parts of all ages.

"In 1954, after nine years in rep, I joined a political magazine. It was a political publication at the height of the Cold War and focused on the Eastern bloc and Asia. The East Coast floods had struck the year before and had badly affected my parents. I needed to be able to reach them and spend time with them at weekends.

"In 1969 I went on to a better job at a Unilever company as Personal Assistant to the Director of Research and Development and I became editor of their house magazine. Then in 1978 the department relocated to Newcastle and Unilever quite accurately concluded that I did not want to move there. Also the lease of my Georgian flat in Islington was coming to an end.

"My mother had died in 1967 10 years after my father. I had built Park Cottage in Church Walk in 1967 and was using it whenever I could. So I now moved in permanently and took a job in Fakenham as a records clerk with Social Services. The area covered included the Burnhams.

"My father ran Overy Mill from 1909 to 1939 when it was sold to the National Trust. And we moved to Burnham Norton. In 1953 I was with them on that dreadful night of the East Coast floods when high tides met devastating winds and the water surge engulfed and destroyed so much of the North Norfolk coast. There was 15ft of water in the mill. Our house in Norton was made of clunch and I can remember sitting on the stairs at the height of the storm as it shuddered with the battering, expecting something to give way any minute. My parents took the view that there was nothing they could do about it and went to bed. The aftermath was nearly as bad as the night itself. Everything was permeated with salt and one never really got rid of it.

"The water stopped at the bridge on the Overy Road largely because the Roys' beehives were washed into the river and got stuck under the bridge, blocking the flood from penetrating further upstream. The railway line between Holkham and Wells was washed away, never to be replaced, and that caused a major change to travel habits in the Burnhams with a considerable growth in the use of motor cars."

Bridget Everitt is very knowledgeable about the history of the Burnhams over the last two millennia.

" Originally called Brunham, situated as it was on the River Brun, the name was changed to Burnham because the Normans could not get their tongues around the original pronunciation. The Saxons fought the Danes at a battle near South Creake and so violent was it that the site bears the name of Bloodgate to this day. The Danes stormed this Saxon fort over the dead bodies of the defenders.

"Lawyer Francis, a well known Burnhams character in his day, I think had a copy of the Burnhams Charter issued by King John and dated 1202 or 1209. The river Burn which had been navigable up to North Creake started to silt up in Elizabethan times."

The characters of yesteryear were as interesting as some of their successors today. Burnham Westgate Hall was built by Sir John Soane on the site of an old farmhouse in co-operation with Thomas Pitt, Baron Camelford, cousin of Prime Minister William Pitt, between 1783 and 1785. Thomas Pitt had been offered the Premiership by King George III in 1783, but turned it down on health grounds. His son, the second Baron, was to become known as the Mad Lord Camelford for his eccentric adventures, first in the Royal Navy and later in politics. He was killed in a duel at the age of 29 in 1804.

"The first occupant of the new Westgate Hall was Sir Mordaunt Martin, a potato baron. He is remembered for the feasts he held on the Green for the village, including the celebration of the Battle of Trafalgar. His son Sir Roger Martin was known as the Wicked Squire. He lived with his housekeeper. His sister married the rector, the Revd Glass. The latter tried valiantly to make Sir Roger, his brother in law, change his ways but was unsuccessful and he shot himself in 1829. He was one of the first suicides to be buried in a churchyard – in the north west corner with unbaptised babies. The law had changed to permit this practice after Lord Castlereagh the Foreign Secretary committed suicide in 1822. The rector's wife moved away in shock and never returned. Sir Roger's housekeeper succeeded to ownership of Westgate Hall and eventually sold it. Later it became a British Legion home for the blind and then a Council owned nursing home. Today it is a fine private house once more."

Ena Mason (née Snelling)

Ena Snelling's paternal grandfather lived in a cottage opposite Londis and survived well into his 80s. Her father, Philip, was one of four brothers and, with his brother Tom, had a butcher's business in Burnham Market. His brother Jack was a butcher in London and the youngest brother, Tim, had a smallholding in Kent.

Ena explains, "The Snelling butchers' shop was situated on the car park outside Lime Tree House, renamed Market House after the lime trees were removed. The shop was previously owned by Wilsons for whom my father worked before he took it over.

"My father was straightlaced and Chapel and married a happy go lucky cockney. He first met my mother, Nellie Clarke, when she was visiting her aunt Caroline, wife of Charles Wright, one of the butchers at Burnham Market. My father was friendly with her cousin George Wright and determined at their first meeting with Nellie that he was going to marry her. There was no work in London, particularly in the 1930s, and Nellie's father walked to Burnham Market in search of work.

Old Burnham Market

35

"Her mother had already moved to the village with her two sons. There were five butchers' shops in the village at the time. Charlie Wright's shop was next to the Lord Nelson; Dews had a pork butcher in Front Street; Barkers was where Howells now stands and with its slaughterhouse attached to the house next to the shop; Billy Pull near the Hoste Arms; and Snellings with our slaughterhouse in Clifton House Yard.

"We lived at Aviaries in the Market Place and I used to attend cookery lessons in the old village hall until the stove got too hot and set fire to the ceiling. After that we went to Wells Central School for our cookery lessons, driven by George Hubbard in one of his coaches at about 15 mph. He would hoot at every corner.

"We were never bored as children in the village and there was plenty to do for both children and grown ups. Mostly we had to make our own entertainment, but there was the Cosy Cinema where seats were 3d up to 1/6d. If we sat in the most expensive seats we thought we were royalty.

"The Girl Guides were run by the two Misses Goodman and meetings were held in St Edmunds Room. The Girls' Friendly Society held their meetings in Westgate Rectory from time to time by courtesy of the Reverend Joyce. There were picnics at Overy and we always had the skipping rope or whipping tops handy. There was old time dancing in the village hall. Father was strict and would not let us go to dances, while Mother was more indulgent and did let us go. We had respect for both of them.

"My father was on the Docking district council and the Burnham Market parish council. He played the piccolo and we have a photo of him doing so and dated 1913. In 1914 he became a special constable. He was in the war reserve in 1940 and joined the police force full time in 1948. He was a big impressive man, six feet tall and knew the village trouble makers. The most notorious of these was Jack Marsh whose evasion of capture while being chased by the police was legendary.

"Father played bowls, cricket, football, and collected coins. There were two police houses in the village, one in Church Walk and the other in Creake Road, although we never lived in either. He died in 1959.

"Among the characters in the village was Arnold Lightheart. He sold fresh fish from a hand cart and would stop at every pub on his way to Burnham from Wells. He would leave his cart at the Aviaries while he went for a drink in the Rose and Crown. On many an occasion our cats would help themselves to a cod or some such fish and bring it into our house. My mother would wash it down and place it back in the cart. Another character was Frairy who cycled from Wells with an attached dilly cart from which he sold cockles and mussels and samphire on a Saturday."

In 1921 the population of the Burnhams was 1853 of whom 849 lived in Burnham Westgate, 476 lived in Overy, 333 in Sutton, 109 in Norton and 86 in Deepdale.

"There were many young people around in the 1920s and 30s as families tended to be much larger in those days. Some of the families living in Sands cottages, situated at Pluck Row, had many children. They lived in two-bedroom cottages and there was a strong sense of community and family solidarity which kept them going through hard times.

"The streets were always full of children playing as there were few cars to endanger us. However, most children seldom went out of the village. There would be school treats to Wells where we took part in races on the beach and had memorable teas. George Hubbard drove us on these occasions. We would be excited and anxious to get there and we would urge him to speed up.

"The Goosebec flowed on the surface along Front Street until it was diverted underground before the War. The children playing in the street when the Goosebec was flowing had to wear water boots. The street was full of occupied houses and there were 14 shops. Some of the houses in Front Street had no back entrances so all garbage and nightsoil had to be carried through

Wells next the Sea

37

the houses to the front door to await collection.

"The train service from Burnham station played an important part in village life. We could buy an excursion to London on a Sunday for 5/- return. Crops and cattle were moved by train and every Monday there was a cattle market in the village. Cattle, sheep and pigs went to the cattle market in the yard behind the Hoste.

"Christmas time is the big event for butchers. It meant many hours of preparation to achieve the fine display of Christmas poultry and meat hung outside our shop. Every year Mrs Harby who lived at Rest Harrow in Friars Lane would put on a nativity play. She was a fine, moneyed lady and my grandfather was her gardener.

"Mother carried on running the shop until 1951 when she fell ill and could do so no more."

Lime Tree House was bought by Mrs Buxton, a rather grand lady, one of whose granddaughters was to become the second wife of Lord Wakeham after his first wife had been killed in the Brighton bomb. Mrs Buxton decided that a butchers' shop in such close proximity to her house was inappropriate and when it was put up for auction by its owner Lawyer Francis, she outbid my father and bought the shop for, I think, £400 with the express purpose of demolishing it.

"With it went other well loved features of the village. There was a photographer's shop built of wood on the car park. The Salvation Army used to play outside Lime Tree House every Sunday night. All this and the lime trees have now gone and Burnham Market is the poorer for it.

"The station was bombed during the war. I can remember it was a Sunday night and the Salvation Army band was playing. Everyone watched a plane come over and drop a bomb in the field near the station. It was trying to get the railway line and I saw the bomb fall. Until then we did not realise that the plane was German.

"In 1947 I met George Mason and we married in 1950. He worked for the railway and we lived at Station House which was later to become the Railway Inn. George had won his pilot wings during the war and was a keen all round sportsman. After we had been married for 10 years George's work took us to Dereham. He died at the early age of 41. I had no widow's pension and went to work in the local factories. The range of products made in Dereham in those days included bomb cases under Government contracts and clocks. But one by one they closed. I have continued to live in Dereham but still have some friends in the Burnhams. Many others, like myself have moved away."

John Utting

1832 - 1914 Fakenham to Burnham Market - The Uttings

John Utting's great grandfather, Richard, born in 1832, founded a boot making business in Fakenham. He and his wife Susannah had 10 children, all of whom were educated at Fakenham School. Their youngest son, Frederick, was to be post master at Watton. The fifth son, Albert George, became Registrar and Clerk to Bircham and Stoughton, Solicitors. William became manager of James Lamberts grocers of Snettisham, and Herbert a tailor in Fakenham.

One of Richard Utting's brothers, William Orris Ebbage Utting, had left for Walsall in Staffordshire to seek his fortune

John Utting

in the mid 1800s. He owned a public house and became a builder, returning to Fakenham with his team of workmen in the 1880s to build Coronation Street style houses. Lichfield Street, Walsall Terrace and Birmingham Terrace are testimony to his Midland connections. He owned a brick works at Claypits. When he died in 1916 he is reputed to have had over 100 grandfather clocks. He is buried in Fakenham churchyard in Queens Road.

Richard's eldest son, Reginald Arthur, who was to be John's grandfather, was destined for the boot business but decided it was not for him. He was apprenticed instead to Joseph Baker, ironmonger of Norwich Street, Fakenham, in 1872. The sign over the shop was a black kettle. The apprenticeship certificate survives in good condition and is signed by Reginald Utting and his father in copperplate writing which, when one considers that they both left school at 13, is a

39

remarkable commentary on the standards of the day. The boot making family business was joined by another brother of Reginald's, Richard Utting.

John Utting takes up the story:

"My grandfather became manager of Joseph Baker's ironmonger but when the latter's son, William, came into the business he left and set up his own ironmonger shop with his brother William. They took over the C. T. Baker of Holt branch in Fakenham at the top of Bridge Street opposite where National Westminster bank now stands in the Market Place. Hayes and Storr, solicitors, had a photo of this shop in their waiting room. It showed the golden key sign which hung outside to tell those who could not read that this was the shop to go to for their hardware. That original shop sign is now in the Gas Works Museum in Fakenham.

"After a while the brothers split up. William took the grocers and post office at Hempton and my grandfather took over the Baxter & Co. ironmongers where part of Aldiss is now, next to Currys. His father's boot business was flourishing and he had built four houses in 1886 called Victoria Terrace in Queens Road – renamed by Reginald Senior, when supplying the street names, from its earlier name of Cemetery Lane. My grandfather lived in the house nearest the town, which is where my father, Reginald Arthur Junior, an only child, was born.

"There were riots in Fakenham in the late 1800s when the common land was enclosed. The rioters burned the town pump in the Market Place and Joseph Baker replaced it with a metal one. This destroyed wooden pump had finger pointers showing distances to Norwich and elsewhere and its remains after the fire were made into a counter for the shop at Joseph Baker ironmongers. This was later destroyed when the shop burnt down.

"My father left school at 13 able to write very clearly. For two years he sat on a stool at Bircham and Stoughton, solicitors, writing some of their letters. On his first day with the firm he was to meet Elija Sutherland of Brancaster at the Great Eastern station in Fakenham and carry his bag to the solicitors' office. Later he carried it back to the station and was rewarded with not even a farthing for his effort. Mr Sutherland owned the Jolly Sailors at Brancaster and the Rose and Crown at Burnham Market. He lived at The Rest in London Street, Brancaster, and owned many properties including the Cosy Cinema built in Herrings Lane in 1913. My father concluded that Mr Sutherland was not the only one who was tight with money. After two years at the solicitors he realised they had forgotten to pay him once a year. He left and joined my grandfather in the ironmongers business.

"Market day each Thursday brought the farmers into Fakenham from far and wide and the Burnham farmers got to know the Uttings well in the course of business and conviviality. By 1913 the Uttings decided to open a branch in Burnham Market where trade at the time was in a state of flux. The village was still reeling from the effects of the arrival of International Stores - the equivalent of a Tesco opening today - who had earlier bought out the long established family grocer Walter Butcher, Inglewood and Sunnyside where two houses of that name today stand on the north side of the Green. They had barns and land extending up Herrings Lane.

"International Stores divided the shop, occupied the part nearest to the now Fishes Restaurant and let the other half to the Searles, grocers and drapers, whose main shop was where the White House Bookshop is now. But by 1913 the Searles' business was in serious trouble having overstocked. Mr Searle had made the mistake of mixing local government politics with business. Apart from dividing his clientele it distracted him from running his business efficiently. Most of his stock was sold but bankruptcy was avoided. The sale took place in the Cosy Cinema in Herrings Lane.

"My father had an FN Belgium motorbike which he had bought from the owner of Cranmer Hall, whom he knew through the Fakenham Rifle Club of which they were both members. To buy it he had walked from Fakenham to Cranmer Hall. Then at the auction of the Searles' goods in 1913 he bought Daniel Searle's BSA motorbike which was to play an important part in an incident in his life a year or so later.

"My father wrote to the Searles asking if they were giving up. However, they said they had nowhere else to go but would draw in their horns by relinquishing the lease on the shop rented from International, and concentrate on drapery with their grocer's business in the White House shop. The irony is that a year later when war broke out their stock could have been worth a lot of money to them."

The shop vacated by the Searles was available and it became Uttings ironmongers. "My father lodged during the week where Abbotts now stands. This was part of two Claytons family shops, the other being the present Stubbings fruit shop. At the time there were glass houses and an extensive produce growing area at the back. He returned home on Sundays to Fakenham on the BSA motorbike. My father and grandfather brought in a wagon load of stock from Fakenham and were in business in Burnham Market from 2nd February 1914.

"During the First World War my father volunteered with his friend Harold Womack, one of the sons of the Womack landlord of the Hoste Arms who were also carriage and trap painters. The management of the Utting shop was handed to Ruben West whose family had lived in Market House, known in those days as Lime Tree House. My grandfather came over from Fakenham every market day, which was Monday in Burnham Market, to keep an eye on his Burnham Market branch.

"The Public Hall in Herrings Lane doubled as the Cosy Cinema. It showed silent films in black and white and the lady pianist would speed up her playing when the horses started to gallop. It was built by Charlie Barnes, a fairground showman, for the owner Elija Sutherland. Electricity was generated by a fairground steam engine parked at the rear entrance of Market House. Charlie's sister, Sally Thompson, lived in Overy Staithe and made ice cream in the 1920s, 30s and 40s. Her husband sold this around the villages in a converted Singer car with the message painted on the side 'patronised by the medical profession'. This referred to one of her customers who was a doctor. One Whitsun in the 1930s my parents and I met Charlie Barnes, Mrs Rose Sutherland and her two sons who were all with the fair at the Kursaal in Southend.

"In 1914 my father met and started courting Maud Playford."

Maud Playford and her sisters Grace and Blanche

The Playfords

"My grandfather on my mother's side, Alfred John Playford, was born in 1868 and died in 1929. He lived with his parents at Fakenham Road, Docking, opposite the Old King William pub. They were bakers and had an off licence. My grandfather married Alice Grace Tinker born in 1867 and who died in 1951. Her parents were millers and bakers and had a windmill at South Wootton. The Mill House is still there.

"When they married in the 1880s he bought the house, shop and bakery in Front Street from Erasmus Greenwood who also owned the post mill in Bellamy's Lane. Mr

Greenwood moved to Stanley House on the west side of Burnham Stores now known as Londis. My grandparents had three daughters. The youngest of them, Allie, was to be my mother and she lived until 1980 when she died aged 84. The other two were my aunts Grace and Blanche.

"My grandfather preferred farming to baking and rented the Brancaster Staithe farm from Simms Reeve of Brancaster Hall until 1912 when it was taken back by Simms Reeve. The barn next to Staithe House had seen many a harvest supper in the meantime. My grandfather moved to South Wootton and rented Reffley farm which had previously been farmed by his brother in law William

Alfred John Playford

Tinker. My mother recalled that the first year at Reffley was so wet that not a single shock of corn was harvested. The Reffley Brethrens Chapel was situated in a wooded pasture and my grandfather was invited to join the Brethren for a meal and special punch once a year as the tenant farmer. There were stone lions outside the Chapel and I can remember sitting on them at the age of six. Both my grandfather and I caught flu that year and he died from it. The Carr stone farmhouse is still there and a school stands where the dairy and cowsheds used to be .

"After my grandfather's death there were no male heirs to carry on farming and all the stock was sold including my pony, Merryboy. This was the end of any dreams I had of becoming a farmer. My mother and her two sisters had been left to run the baker's shop in Burnham Market when my grandparents moved to Ruffley in 1912. Aunt Grace was in the shop, selling bread, flour and corn, aunt Blanche ran the house and bakehouse and my mother was out on the bread rounds. In the First World War she covered Burnham Thorpe, Overy, Norton, Deepdale and Brancaster Staithe. She called on the Cooks and their cottages at Sussex farm. One of her customers in the cottages was Mrs Langley with her newborn son Frank who lives at Crabbe Castle, and daughter Mrs M. Curry of Beacon Hill Road.

"She delivered the bread from an open cart pulled by a pony. Her ponies were kept in Friar Ruin field and as she went to collect them each morning the German prisoners from the Maltings in Station Road were being marched round the Friars to Burnham Norton to clean out the marsh dykes. She was a young lady and it was a little unnerving for her as the Germans would say things to her in their language."

The First World War

"My father and his best friend Harold Womack volunteered for the army in the motor machine gun corps. This consisted of Lewis guns mounted on motorcycles with side cars and was later to become the tank corps. They were sent for training at Elveden, Lord Iveagh's estate near Thetford.

"The development of the tank was top secret at the time and there was a special siding where the earliest models were delivered, camouflaged and with 'water tanks for Mesopotamia' painted on the sides. This is why they were called tanks. My father was soon promoted to sergeant and was allowed home to Fakenham when they had time off. Just before they were to be shipped to France they were all confined to barracks. However, my father was determined not to lose his BSA motorbike and absented himself to ride it to Fakenham, catching the train back to Thetford.

"On his return to camp he was arrested, his stripes removed and he was designated for court martial. The proceedings were pursued on arrival in France but the officer representing him pleaded that a British soldier cannot be tried on foreign soil for a crime committed in the UK. Nothing more was done and he worked his way up the ranks again, ending the war as a staff sergeant attached to HQ under General Fuller and General Martel. He owed this post to the fact that he could type. In 1917 he typed out the first battle order ever to be issued where tanks went into action en masse. This order is now in the Tank Corps museum.

"We had the Christmas card - also in the Tank Corps museum - sent to my mother in 1918 from Staff Sergeant Utting. His name is on it with Bombadier Wells, the famous boxer who was also the man who struck the gong to introduce Rank films. He came out of the army in 1919 and wanted to marry. Fishes was a private house at the time and he bought it from Walter Barker the butcher for £1000 which was a lot of money in 1919. He also had to spend money on it, retaining Monuments of Fakenham to do the work. This included turning part of the ground floor into a shop and installing a new staircase and new dining room, kitchen, pantry and toilet at the rear.

1920 – 1942

"My mother and father were married in 1920 in South Wootton church and they moved to live at Fishes. My aunt Blanche was due to be married in 1923 and the baker's shop and house in Front Street were sold to George Trett who had worked for my grandfather. The Docking bakehouse and shop were sold to my grandmother's brother Charles Tinker.

"Fishes had three bedrooms and sitting room upstairs and also an attic. I, their only child, was born in the room furthest east on the first floor in 1923. Father

Blanche Playford and Reg Utting – peace celebrations 1919

gave up Inglewood which Uttings had rented since their arrival in Burnham Market in 1914 but later rented it again.

"In 1919 my father bought his first car. It was a one cylinder 1903 Rover which was sold to him by a vicar at Hunstanton for £90. In the 1920s he bought 1-cwt kegs of carbide, 20 at a time, and coming into the Kings Lynn docks. Hitherto bikes had used oil lamps with a wick but carbide gave off a gas when mixed with water and this was lit to shed the light. On Saturday mornings during the winter I used to help his errand boy fill 1-lb tins of carbide from the kegs, having a 1lb weight and an empty tin on one side of the scales. The tins were long and narrow and we had to bang the bottom on the floor to get a lb of carbide into them. The empty tins were returned for a 1d refund. Occasionally we would load carbide into a Lyle's syrup tin and make our own big bang for a laugh, by mixing water with the carbide and then banging the lid on. The Rover car was sold in the 1920s for £2 to Couzens and Fryett, threshing machine owners who used the engine to drive the chaff cutter.

"The older allotment holders used to have what we called dilly carts. These were two-wheeled hand carts in which they collected horse manure from the street. Like many of my friends I became one of the Hold Ye Boys (see Harry Farrow chapter).

"My best pal was the grandson of blacksmith Augustus Kendall, Leonard Kendall (Thomas Augustus Leonard Kendall - TALK). Their blacksmith's shop was in the yard up from Anna's along the Hoste Arms wall. Leonard's father Thomas was chauffeur for Dr Hamil at Burnham House. He then worked for Mr George Hubbard as bus and lorry driver. Augustus sold the house, blacksmith's shop and buildings to George Hubbard during the recession to keep his son Thomas in work. But after owning the property Thomas was given notice and his job given to a single man, Thomas Smith.

"Thomas Kendall was out of work with two children living at Fern Cottage. He became chauffeur to General Cavendish at Model Farm, Peterstone, and after their death moved to the Cavendishes' daughter's at Frimley Lodge near Camberley. She was married to Captain Maxwell. When Thomas Kendall worked at Peterstone my father sold him a Rudge Whitworth bicycle which his family still had in the 1950s. Jock Monro was another character who worked for General Cavendish and had come to the area with the Lovat Scouts. Jock had a second jacket which he would hang up at some visible spot to give the general the impression that he was working in the vicinity when he was in fact in The Victoria at Holkham.

"Death and recession alter families' lives and although we children were unaware of the recession as such, looking back there were some very hard times for parents to bring up their families. The First World War was just the curtain raiser to the privations of the recession to come in the 1930s.

"Meanwhile I started school in Burnham Market where the Olivers' lighting business is now situated in North Street. Mrs Lottie Witton was the long time teacher of the infants. She lived with a lodger, Mr Teak, in Front Street in the cottage named after her. This has since been substantially converted. In her day there was no staircase, just a ladder. Miss Smith was head of the girls' school on the east side of the site. The boys' site was on the west side. The boys' teacher was Miss Gower, later to become Mrs Bird and later still Mrs Hall.

"Each year the school doctor used to come and examine us with our mothers present. When I was eight or nine he diagnosed that I should have my tonsils out and the operation was performed on the kitchen table at home with my mother holding the dish into which they were deposited by Dr Sharp. He was assisted by Dr Hicks as anaesthetist who for many years practised in Wells where he was doctor, surgeon and anaesthetist.

"At the age of nine the boys went into the next class where Mr Walter Newall was teacher. He lived with his mother and sister opposite Polstede Place. He had been in the First World War and his father had been station master at Fransham. Walter Newall caned me repeatedly for being left handed and forced me to sit with my left hand behind my back so I could not use it for writing. I am still left handed for everything except writing. The classroom was heated by a coal fire in the winter and when we returned for the winter term we would find all the desks turned round so Mr Newall could sit with his back to the fire.

"At the age of 11 the boys moved to the Headmaster, Mr Keeble, for lessons. During holidays and after school we sometimes played on Cook's Meadow at Eastgate House where the two Misses Cook lived for 60 years. This is where the Cubs would meet in the summer time. In the winter we would meet in the village hall (the Hut) - a First World War army hut at St Ethelbert's church north of the ruins.

"The Misses Cook were benefactors to the village and kind to successive generations in their generous openness of the house and fields. We used to catch newts in their pond and throw sticks up into the conker trees in season. The Trett's horses grazed in their field. Old Mr Petts was their handy man who kept up the garden and tennis court and toiled loyally for years. They lived to be 99 and 96 and are buried next to each other in Norton cemetery. Their father had farmed at Sussex farm and their brother who died from oyster poisoning farmed at Deepdale. A close friend of the Misses Cook was the daughter of Dr Hamill of Burnham House. She became Mrs Anthony Everitt and lived at Shammer farm, North Creake.

"At the age of 11 I started at Fakenham Secondary School and would catch the 8.20 train from Burnham Market each morning, changing at Wells. For the first part of the journey we travelled in old Great Eastern carriages with no corridors. Each compartment was heated by a cast iron pipe and the initiation ceremony was to be pushed under the seat while the others jumped on it. I would return home coal black and my mother would ask whatever I had been doing to get in such a state. It was not long before I was joining in the initiation rites on others and jumping on the seats. The second part of the journey from Wells to Fakenham used carriages which had corridors and toilets. We found a way to switch the 'vacant' sign on the door to 'engaged' from the outside.

The discomfort of other passengers who waited outside and banged on the door to encourage the occupant to get on with it, caused us some innocent pleasure.

"There were boys and girls from the villages around who made the daily trip with me to Fakenham Secondary School as it was then called. Some, such as Miss Gidney, had long journeys before they caught the train. She came from Bircham and this meant cycling to Docking station before 8 a.m. and home again after 6 p.m. which is more than four miles each way. Peter Stone, whose father was the station master at Docking, Spooner and his sister whose father was headmaster of Docking School, and Basil John Mason joined the train at Docking. Basil Mason was later to become Sir John (Basil) Mason CB,FRS and had a distinguished career as a leading meteorologist and environmentalist. He was President of the Royal Meteorological Society from 1968 to 1970.

"James Tuck got on at Stanhoe, and Ogden who lived at Brancaster joined the train at Burnham Market. From Burnham my companions also included Brian, Barry and Biddy Rowland, Arnold Harvey and Anna Baldry. From

Burnham Thorpe there were Hugh Algar, John Parnell, who was later to become Station Master at Kings Lynn, Ada Parnell and Tony Sutherland. I well remember being held out of the window of the moving train by Brian Rowland and Spooner. Each grabbed hold of a leg and pushed me head first through the window on the land side of the train as we crossed the bridge over Freeman Street on the way from Holkham station to Wells. The guard was looking out on the sea side. I stared at the road as we crossed it and think of that experience every time I see the now disconnected bridge where the road from Burnham forks to the Wells quay.

Fakenham

"There were two railway stations at Fakenham and we would terminate at the eastern one on the Norwich Road. This was a good walk to the school now renamed Fakenham College. In the rain our gaberdine macs over our shorts were no protection and we would arrive soaking wet and, as always, too late for assembly. Coming into Burnham on the return journey, if someone threw your cap out of the train it could mean walking half way to Thorpe meadows alongside the track to retrieve it. We arrived back in Burnham Market at 5.30 p.m. Then we had to do our homework.

"The Rowland brothers' father, William Domville Rowland, had an antique shop in Front Street. Queen Mary used to call in her maroon Daimler from Sandringham from time to time. Mrs Rowland was the district nurse and Mr Rowland would help me with my maths homework. He could always get the answer right but it was the bit in the middle that caused the problem tracking how he got there. I did not like school much although I took the prizes in my classes for history and geography. I was not much good at French but with Mr Rowland's help I did all right in maths. I liked football but not cricket and was quite good at woodwork. I still have the stool I made at the time.

Albert Rainsbury from Burnham Norton was another school boy at Burnham School and he was always the one to be caught. He was caned by Mr Keeble the headmaster more often than the rest of us because he seemed to be the easiest target. He now lives at Wells.

"When I left school there was never any doubt that I would go into the family business. Burnham Market had oil lamps and never had gas. We had oil lamps until the 1930s when installation of electricity came to the village. It did not come to Stanhoe until after the Second World War. Our shop had the first petrol pump beside the east window, supplied by Shell who

Utting's Ironmongers - the first petrol pump

49

had a depot at Docking. The 500-gallon tank was on the car park. The petrol pump had two glass vessels each holding half a gallon, one being full of petrol. Then a brass lever would be pulled across and one would empty while pumping the other one full by a semi rotary pump. Before the installation of the pumps we sold petrol in two-gallon cans.

"Pratts, which was the original name for Esso, had a depot in Polestede Place. They supplied George Hubbard's two pumps for his bus and coach business at Anna's and Mr Bell's two pumps at his garage which is now the Roman Catholic church. Lawyer Francis owned what is now the car park in front of Fishes on which there was a butchers' shop, cottages and Mr Clamp's photographic studio housed in a wooden building. In the late 1930s it was taken down and moved to Overy beach as a hut. In the west display window of the studio there was a large photo of the Duke of Tek, Queen Mary's brother, on a horse taken outside Model farmhouse at Peterstone. Lawyer Francis lived at Clifton House and had his office at Estcourt House in Front Street.

"There were over 100 beach huts at Overy Staithe in the 1930s on the sand hills each side of the harbour entrance. Three local families from Overy Staithe, the Thompsons, the Lanes and the Haines, made their living carting supplies to the beach huts. In the hard times Uttings received a motor boat in payment of a bill and we part exchanged it for a Morris Major through Peter Walsingham's grandfather who was manager for G. F. Rose's garage at Wells. Peter now has shops in Staithe Street, Wells.

"My father was caught in a swindle during the recession. A farmer whom he knew and who was a customer came into the shop at 1.10 p.m. on a Friday, claiming that he had missed the bank and needed cash to pay his farm workers. Could Reggie Utting cash the cheque for him? It bounced and my father ruefully accepted that he had paid the farm wages for a week. He always told me that you should never lend money. Either give it and forget about it or refuse it as friendships could suffer.

"We never took proper holidays. At Whitsun we would go to Clacton or Felixstowe in the Morris Major car on the Sunday and return on Monday night. My uncle and aunt Blanche who lived in Wallasey would rent a beach hut for two weeks on Overy beach. As a young boy I would stay with them and my parents would walk down to stay on August bank holiday Saturday night, returning home on the Monday night.

"Fisher Haines of Overy Staithe was asked by my father to build a hut for us on Overy beach. The agent for Holkham Estates had to be consulted and the site was chosen near the one known as the Seagull. Fisher Haines started to build the two bedroom bungalow, but very slowly. William Allen who had worked for my father since leaving school, and was a handyman, finished building it. His parents were marshmen living at Norton.

"The Roys established a trout farm in 1937/8 near their mill in Overy Road. There were three brothers, Philip, Sydney and Gladstone. The system was concrete troughs running south to north and Uttings supplied the perforated galvanised sheeting at either end to let the water through but keep the trout in. This worked well until some evacuees from Shoreditch, who had never

Reg Utting and Baden Dew (with violin)
1935 Silver Jubilee

seen fish like this in captivity, let them out into the river.

"My father and my grandfather eventually had three shops: the original one in Fakenham, at Burnham Market, and at Docking which was rented off Barclays Bank. My father died aged 80 in 1969. My grandfather died in 1946 aged 88. My grandparents, parents and aunts were a lovely happy family and I cannot remember any trouble between them. As the only grandson I was spoilt.

"In the early 1930s, during the recession, we had converted a Morris vehicle, which had been used to carry game on estate shoots, into a mobile shop. William Allen and Sidney Wakefield were our first roundsmen. We supplied the surrounding villages on set days of the week. On Mondays we served the fishermen at Brancaster, Tuesday was Stanhoe and Bircham, Wednesday Overy Town, Thursday Overy and Burnham Thorpe, and Friday the Creakes, Shammer and Burnham Sutton. Sometimes we would go miles for 6d.

" Some of our customers' farm workers were paid on a Friday and my father would have to go on Saturday mornings by car to Burnham Overy, Overy Town and Burnham Thorpe to collect money from some of those customers who had purchased goods from the mobile shop as by Thursday they had no money.

"The advent of World War II brought its problems early on. A number of men who worked for us joined the TA initially before joining up into the regular forces. The war memorial records the names of the men who were killed in action and two of them worked for us - Cyril Snell and George Barwick. Cyril Snell went to fight the Japanese and was one of the first to be killed. Denny Rix, father of Brian Rix the builder, returned from Japanese prison camps at the end of the war. When Denny Rix and Albert Groom were called up it brought problems of how to cover their rounds as I was going to be the next to be called up.

"We had to improvise. The villages relied on paraffin but this was rationed. We had to look for school leavers as drivers who were too young for immediate call up but who were old enough to drive a particular type of vehicle. The age for driving a three-wheeled vehicle was a year younger than for a four-wheeler. We advertised in the *Eastern Daily Press* and bought a James three-wheeler van for £40 from a man at Bircham.

"In 1937 or thereabouts we heard of a secondhand Morris 18 which was owned by a butcher in Norwich who had fallen out with his bookmaker and needed to make a quick sale. I remember it had big chrome lamps and the asking price was £140. A new one cost approx. £300. My father offered £70 but the butcher turned it down. However, he later changed his mind and accepted it – presumably the pressure from the bookmaker helped the decision. We really looked after that vehicle waxing it regularly. We decided it was too big in the war. My father sold it but it was later in an accident on the bends at Holkham – a sad end.

"So in 1940 we ordered a new and recently introduced Ford Anglia from Hill and Osborne for £130 and a Ford 10 van. However, Mr Hill contacted us before the Anglia was delivered to say that the price had gone up by £10 and were we still interested. We agreed to that. We did not get the van until after the war. The car was delivered in an open rail truck from Dagenham to Burnham Market station. We sold it 10 years later for £300 – the only time we ever made money on a vehicle sale.

"Mr Osborne was a very clever engineer. The clutch of our Morris van went when I was trying to turn round at Gravel Hill, Overy Town on the Burnham Overy Road in 1941. I walked to Mr Roy's at Union Mill and Mr Yaxley brought a farm horse with trace harness to pull the van over the hump. Then he waited at the hump bridge and pulled the van over that too. I was then able to drive the van with the clutch slipping to Hill and Osborne's garage. They pushed the van over the inspection pit where Mr Osborne disconnected the gear box from the engine, taking off the clutch plate. He told me to go to Gilbert White's chemist and buy corks of a certain size. Mr Osborne fitted the corks in the clutch plate cutting them to the right height. Then having put all the parts together I was driving the van again that day.

"In World War II units of the Local Defence Volunteers were formed in the Burnhams. These were later to be named by Churchill as the Home Guard. The first duty given to the younger volunteers was for one to cycle to the searchlight battery at Westgate Farm in Ringstead Road, staying with the soldiers in their army huts all night. If they were in action they watched the beam of the searchlight trying to pick out enemy aircraft. My night was Saturday.

"If the invasion came during the night it was my job to cycle to the post office in Burnham Market to wake Mr Frederick Stimpson, the Post Master. He would then contact the other LDV troops who had telephones and each of them would contact others who had not. Then we all turned out with 12 bore shotguns, .22 rifles and whatever came to hand. The LDV used to meet in Mr Shearer's field in Herrings Lane on Sunday mornings. Headquarters was at Clifton House."

1942 – 1973 and beyond

"In 1942 I was called up to Rhyl in North Wales. I had opted for the tank corps so they put me in the Artillery. I left Burnham on the 7 a.m. train and had to change at Heacham, Kings Lynn, Peterborough, Rugby, Crewe and Chester, reaching the Sunny Vale holiday camp in Rhyl at 9 p.m. There I was told the cookhouse was closed for the night and there was nothing to eat. On the following day I was vaccinated and inoculated.

"I did my initial training at Rhyl before being posted to the 12/25 battery of the 25th Field Regiment Royal Artillery at Wiseton near Bawtry. This was the home of Brigadier General Laycock. He was in charge of the Commandos and we stayed in the lofts above his stables. I also did a four-week signalling course at Nostell Priory. I can remember peeling potatoes there during the night with other gunners, helping the cooks fill dustbins full in the kitchen of the Priory, where coke ranges gave off noxious fumes making us feel very unwell. It was winter time with snow so we kept all the doors and windows closed.

"However, one always remembers the good times. The regiment moved to Aldershot and Crookham before embarking for Normandy with my battery in landing craft. We landed on the beaches on Gold Beach at Arromanches as part of the second army. The landing reminded me of Overy beach.

"I was one of two driver operators in 'Roger Able' Observation Post (O.P.) crew. The other was Eric Manley whom I first met at Wiseton. We went all through the war together from then on. He came from Wombwell near Barnsley and we remained firm friends until he died in 2001. Ron Hodgson was our driver and Captain O'Brien our O.P. officer.

"Mostly we were in a bren gun carrier but when supporting armoured brigades or divisions sometimes we were in Churchill or Sherman tanks. Artillery could seldom see their targets and relied on directions to fire from Observation Posts. From June 1944 until May 1945 we worked with over 40 formations covering 2100 miles. In one of the advances in August we were attached to the rifle brigade, part of 11th Armoured Division near Le Beny Bocage. The next morning, advancing with the infantry, taking the village of Presles, all was going well and we were being kissed by the French men and women and being given calvados to drink. But moving on to higher ground we came under heavy shell fire from German tanks of the Weiss SS Panzers1021. Other Panzers had retaken Presles. So we made a kind of circle like the old cowboy and indian films with anti-tank and self-propelled guns pointing out of the circle and the infantry digging their slit trenches.

"The six-pounder anti-tank gun next to us opened fire, giving our position away and straightaway receiving a direct hit, killing all their crew, wounding Captain O'Brien and Ron our driver. On the other side of us the open topped Sherman tank moved back and took a direct hit. Eric Manley and I were the only two artillery O.P.s left to send fire orders for the rest of that day and the next to the army group of artillery near Beny Bocuse. We also directed Typhoon aircraft to the Panzer tanks. Being surrounded we could not evacuate our wounded and Ron our driver died during the night. During the second day British troops broke through to us. Eric and I lived to fight on during the winter in Holland. Eric was awarded the Military Medal for his part in the action .

"Under a new captain we moved on to Holland and the River Maas. We made some good friends among the Dutch families we met and I still keep in touch.

"From Holland on 25th March 1945 we crossed the Rhine in a US Buffalo. We then crossed the Elbe on a raft on 30th April, attached to 6th Airborne Canadian Division and on 2nd May we were the first to meet the Russians in the last devastating days of the war on the Wismar–Rostock coast road. We saw the Baltic at 7.30 p.m. It was all brought back to us recently when the TV sequence *The World at War* showed the Russians capturing Berlin and Hitler's death. The Army Information Unit had arrived in Wismar on 3rd May 1945 and we replayed the part of the link up. There am I with Eric Manley on the screen. Photos were taken by Captain Matheson with a German camera on 2nd May 1945, filmed at the rendezvous.

John Utting in January 1945 Brussels

"We moved on to Magdaberg but following the agreement with the Russians and Americans at Yalta we were pulled back to Blankenberg in Germany. We pulled back again to Duderstat near the Hartz mountains. Captain Matheson was developing a club at the Golden Lion Hotel and he offered me a job to help run it.

"I was reluctant but after some persuasion agreed to do it for a week. I shared a bedroom with Sgt Evans and conditions were a vast improvement. There was running water, a bed and a better food supply. The German owner resented us but could do little about it. German bakers used to make sticky buns from NAAFI rations the regiment received and there was local venison and wild boar shot by Capt. Matheson for our evening meal. The German staff were pleased to have a meal each day and this was more important than marks.

"Sometimes ENSA the entertainment unit stayed overnight and dined there. The cellars were full of schnapps and twice a week we would drive our three-ton Bedford truck to the Krops brewery in Kassel, a large bombed town and in the US sector. It took us a day to get there and back because the bridges were down causing endless detours. By arrangement with the US sergeant in charge we would exchange four bottles of schnapps for a three-ton truck load of barrels of beer made from imported hops. We paid for the beer but the sergeant booked it down to an American unit.

"This went on throughout the winter and I stayed until I was demobbed in the spring of 1946. We were sent first to Woolwich and then to Olympia to receive our demob suit in whatever colour fitted, and a trilby hat. We kept our uniform and greatcoats which were all most of us had, having grown out of our own pre-war clothes during the war years.

"It was a bit of a shock coming home to Burnham Market in 1946. I had not been with Norfolk people in the army and found the accent strange – but soon fell back into it. And it was all so quiet after the experiences in Europe. I remembered the first Russian officer we met on 2nd May, who'd had too much schnapps to drink and was showing off his captured Luger pistol. There were five of us in the mess room of a German house and he nearly blew us all to pieces as the bullets ricocheted round the walls. He showed us a handkerchief full of wedding rings he had taken from the fingers of German women as he advanced across Germany.

"However, I was fortunate. I had a happy family, still intact, which is more than many found on returning from the war. My father was getting on for 60 and my mother 54. My grandfather had died in 1946 at the age of 88 and I had two aunts living locally. After two or three years I was made a partner in the business although I continued to do the same hands on work! We had four staff including Denny Rix – Brian Rix the builder's father, who had returned from Japanese captivity.

"In the 1950s I started courting but we had nowhere to live in Burnham Market. My future wife Cis (Lillian) had a wool shop in Staithe Street in Wells. My father bought the plot of land in Station Road at the corner of Angles Lane to build a house for himself and my mother. He paid £350 for it and it attracted comment from Mr Hill of Hill and Osborne that these were Regent Street, London prices. We waited two years whilst planning permission was obtained, the house was built and they moved out of Fishes so we could move in as newly weds. It was all very frustrating. We were married on St Valentine's Day in 1956. Cis's sister took over the running of the wool shop.

"Later I bought Anna's next door to get the warehouse at the back although my mother moved into Anna's in the 1960s. Later we let it to Paul Whittome of the Hoste and sold it in 1990. In 1973 we sold the shop – the day before VAT became law!

"The Cold War helped Burnham Market. Sculthorpe was the leading airfield supplying the Berlin Airlift and the wives of the Americans stationed there filled the houses in and around the village. They seemed to live in housecoats and were used to warm houses. The US officer in charge of weather forecasting lived at Westgate Rectory. He told me he had forecast the weather all over the world but said that the Burnham Market area was the worst to forecast of any he had known. There was a strong demand for Aladdin paraffin heaters to help them keep warm.

"The NHS also benefited employment in the Burnhams when it was introduced soon after the War. Free dental and eye treatment were too good to miss and the demand for spectacles soared. Mr Allen Bell of Overy Staithe had a garage on the site of the present Catholic church. This had been let to Hill & Osborne before the Second World War. During the war it was a gas cleansing centre. He now let it to a firm of spectacle frame makers. The hinges for the frames were made at Overy Staithe by Mr Bell. This gave work for the women and helped Uttings in a small way in that we supplied quires of sandpaper used in polishing the frames. On calling on Mrs Lilley Eke of Burnham Thorpe she forecast at the time that the NHS boom would not last and it was only a matter of time before we would have to pay for all this free dentistry and eye care. And she was right but the Eke family were taking advantage of it before it stopped.

"About the same time Alleys Farm Trailers factory set up where the garage is near the station. This gave work for the men. I think Alleys were the first to produce the three-way tipping trailer. Their production was sent off from Burnham Market by rail.

"The 1960s were bad for Burnham Market. It was all down hill. The cattle market closed as had the cinema. The railway had been partially washed away in the East Coast floods and was further reduced by the Beeching cuts. It closed altogether in 1964. There was no work for youngsters and many shops closed.

"Until 1973 and since the late 1940s I was on the rounds with one of our employees to the Burnhams and to Brancaster Staithe and Town, Creakes, Stanhoe, Peterstone, Shammer and Docking. We worked from 9.30 a.m. to 5.30 p.m. with later hours in the winter, especially during bad weather and snow, sometimes arriving home after 9 p.m. Most of the time I liked the rounds selling and delivering orders from the van. We were always moving about, freed from the confines of the shop. It also meant contact with people in surrounding areas some of whom had difficulty getting out and about.

"My parents were in the shop with our other employees – my father until two days before he died aged 80 in 1968. For another four years and more my wife and I tried to persuade my mother to take life more easily. However, since the Second World War this had been her life, and every working day she was in the shop.

"The only way to stop her working was to sell the business, our house and shop. We sold to Mr and Mrs Cape who moved in on April 1st 1973. My wife and I moved to Angles House in Station Road from which my mother had previously moved to my Forge House next to the shop.

"Since the death of Harold Moorhouse I have been one of the trustees of the charity he stated in his will of which I was an executor. He left a capital sum of approximately £100,000. The charity benefits from the interest and also from the rent of the 31-acre field left in his will. The annual income is about £12,000. The trustees give £2000 each year to both the Friends of Wells Cottage Hospital and the Royal National Institute for the Blind. Part of the rest is dispersed each year to parishioners in Burnham Market who receive on average £50 each.

"During the Gulf War I had a phone call from a Captain Wallis from Woolwich, saying that he had traced three of us who were the surviving veterans of the Battle of Asten. I thought for a moment that as a Z reservist I was being called up, as I had been for the Korean War, even though I was in my 70s. However it proved to be a celebration of the 12/25 Battery 25th Field Regiment, now called the 59th Asten Battery. It gave me the opportunity to travel to Asten in Holland with Eric Manley and Derek Kay for a reunion with my friends there, to see the battlefield and attend a Civic greeting. Also with us were the Officers and NCOs of the 59th Asten Battery from Woolwich. On our return we attended a celebration at Woolwich in the ballroom. The three of us, called the Battle of Asten veterans, were asked by the Master Gunner to pull the cords of the curtains covering the mural of 200 years of the Battery.

"The Battle of Asten earned the regiment battle honours from the 7th US Armoured Division. As the three of us were out of the army we did not know that until 1991.

"I am very interested in the history of the Burnhams and like to contribute to and advise on how things were and how they have developed over seven decades."

Harry Farrow

Harry Farrow was born in Front Street, Burnham Market, in 1924. He went to Burnham school and remembers schoolmaster Mr Newall who played a formative part in many a young life in the village. " He was a man of many parts and as well as being our teacher he was also the Cubs' master and keen on cricket. When the Test matches were on he would come and tell us the score at 1.30 p.m. when they broke for lunch. By that time we would have had our lunch break from 12 to 1.00 p.m. and be back in class.

"The big event every year was the carnival on the sports field. This included the flower show and sports for the children and adults. The children's races were held before tea and then we would all come back for the adults' races. We also held sports in the field opposite the garage in Creake Road, which is now farmed by Mr Stilgoe. In 1936 when I was aged 12, I won a medal there for the tug of war. This was not for pulling but for shouting. I always had a loud voice which I used sometimes out of turn and this would get me into trouble with Mr Keeble, the headmaster of Burnham School. He was able to distinguish my voice from a considerable distance and I was in trouble even when we did not think he was around.

Harry Farrow

"We all had to earn money as soon as possible to contribute to our parents' housekeeping and to be able to afford something extra for ourselves. If you did not work for it in those days you did not get it. So at the age of 11 along with many of my friends in the village I became one of the 'Hold Ye (Holgee or Howjee) boys' who were regular helpers at harvest time. If we worked at the harvest until it was all gathered in we would be paid a bonus. But if we were casual we would not get the bonus.

"The job of the Hold Ye Boys was to lead the wagon horse or walk beside it whilst the corn stooks were forked up to the men standing on top of the four-wheeled wagon pulled by one or two horses. The men stacked the bound shufts together to make the stook and as the cart approached each stook the boy in charge of the wagon shouted 'Hold Ye' so the stooks would be forked on to it. When the wagon reached the elevator the stooks were forked on to it to take them up to the stack. This was worked by a horse or mule going round and round all day. It could only go one way or the elevator would work in reverse.

"You did not become a Hold Ye Boy until you had worked your apprenticeship as an Elevator Boy. We started at about the age of 11 and the job was to keep the horse or mule continually walking round in its circle to elevate the stooks. When there was a gap in the supply of stooks we would stop the animal until the next load arrived.

"Once we had done our stint as elevator boys we could be upgraded to Hold Ye boys at the next harvest. Then in the third year we would be entrusted to be rake boys where we would ride the horse-drawn rake and gather up the loose straw which still had its corn heads attached. When we had raked a pile we would lift the rake and then move on to make the next pile. The men would then come round after us and fork the piles onto the top of the wagon.

"In those days the sugar beet was loaded onto railway wagons and the train would come every evening to take it to the factory in Kings Lynn. This went on throughout the season from October to February and the sound of it was a regular feature of the sounds of the Burnhams.

"When I left school at the age of 14 I was apprenticed to International Stores which was situated next to Fishes Restaurant. The Manager was Alfred Moorhouse. This was in 1938 and my apprenticeship was for three years. In the first year my wages were 10/- per week rising to 15/- in the second year and £1 in the third.

"Groceries were delivered to customers in those days. Bike orders were taken one day and delivered the next in the Burnhams. For Brancaster the orders were collected from the Burnham shop and delivered by the van attached to the Wells shop. The Burnham shop had only a delivery bike and it was quite an effort to deliver a load of groceries by bike to Overy. Parcels had to be tied up in brown paper. Apprentices usually had to do a spell as errand boys before working in the shop but I worked in the shop from the beginning and did not have to do the all weather delivery work.

"I stayed on for a while after completing my apprenticeship and then left to join the NAAFI. Initially this meant cycling to Holkham and later to the airfield at Bircham Newton. I was called up at the end of 1942 and went to Britannia Barracks in Norwich. After infantry training in Northampton I opted to stay in the infantry but I was put into tanks and joined the Royal Armoured Corps at Catterick. Later I was transferred to the 12th Devons which was a batallion attached to the 6th Air Landing Brigade. I was with the anti-tank section using gliders for transportation. When I was demobbed I returned to work for the NAAFI. One of my clearest and saddest memories of the war was, on Beacon Hill, seeing a Wellington bomber flying in low with its navigation lights on ready to land when a German plane stalked it from behind and shot it down. All the crew were killed. We could see it happening yet there was nothing one could do to warn the Wellington or prevent it in any way.

"In pre war days there were three fish and chip shops in the village. Batterbys was in Front Street, Guineys was where Gillys is now on Overy Road, and Robins at the junction of Creake Road and Overy Road at Burnham Ulf which is the shop I bought and renamed Farrows. I was greatly helped in the early days by Mrs Riches, the previous owner of Robins, and by my mother for a number of years. I was to own and run that shop for 35 years until I sold the business in 1984. In those days we sold wet fish as well as fried fish. It took some time to build up the trade but it became a successful business through hard work."

One of Harry Farrow's hobbies is to collect the used postage stamps we get every day but which most of us throw away. These are of value for charity.

Hoste Arms Bowls Club

Left to Right: Ted Parsons, N. Steele, N. Ives, Lawrence, ?, Arminger, Moulton, W. Barker, Warren R. Grint, H. Curson, J. Drake, D. Bower, R. Utting, M. Wright, D. Redcliff, R. Rout

Burnham Norton

Stafford Snell MBE

In the 1930s the Snell family lived opposite the village hall in Burnham Sutton. Stafford was born there in 1935. He has one sister, Valerie. Their father who had four brothers, all of whom were farm workers, and one sister, was born and bred in Burnham Market and their mother came from Grimston. She was in service for many years.

"By the time I went on from Burnham School to Fakenham Grammar School the railway journey with its changeover at Wells had been replaced by a coach service supplied by Jimmy Needs of Fakenham. This was a door to door service and cut out the long walk in all weathers from the railway station on the Norwich road which earlier pupils had to make morning and night.

"My main interest from an early age was gardening and when we moved to Church Walk I was able to satisfy it. At the age of 12 I received my prize possession which I still have and treasure. This is a proper garden spade with a wooden handle which with care, cleaned and oiled, has survived more than half a century of use. We grew a lot of vegetables in the late 40s and early 50s. I had a little cart and collected horse manure from the road to spread on the garden. We used to go to Clifton House to get our added rations. These came in the form of meat pies allocated to agricultural workers to give them strength to grow food for the nation.

"We seldom took holidays. Perhaps one week a year after harvest when a typical programme would be: Burnham Market on Monday when the livestock market sales were held, Kings Lynn on Tuesday, Hunstanton on

Stafford Snell MBE

65

Wednesday, Fakenham on Thursday for market day and at home on Friday with fish and chips for tea. Then the big event of the week was a trip to Norwich on the Saturday. This was a combined shopping and eating expedition. It was the opportunity to buy supplies of clothing and odds and ends before the winter set in, at a time when there was a bit more money in our pockets following the harvest. Then we would go and eat at Purdey's restaurant in Davy Place and have a proper blow out. Towards the end of the day, but not before, we would go to the market when prices for fruit etc. were being knocked down for clearance.

"Despite rationing we ate quite well. There was always a roast on a Sunday and we had stew twice a week – it was always better on the second day – and fish and chips on Fridays from Guineys who also sold potato fritters. We would buy our sweet ration from Mrs Beaver's tiny shop at Burnham Sutton near the church. There was another sweet and fag shop, Gollages, where Humble Pie is now.

"When I left school I went to work for a year at a nursery at Dereham and lived in all week, returning to Burnham at about 2 p.m. on Saturdays. In the summer I would cycle back to Dereham on the Sunday evening, otherwise I would take the train from Wells.

"Then I was called up to the RAF. I had opted for the RAF police but they would not take me unless I was prepared to sign up for longer than three years. So I joined the RAF Medical Service and after initial training at Kirkham near Blackpool was stationed at North Pickenham near Swaffham. They had a sub unit at Tuddenham near Mildenhall and a medical unit, which was me! I had passed my exams and tests by then and had my own sick room and driver. If sick parade revealed significant problems I would take them to Mildenhall where there were extensive facilities. Whilst I had to sift out any malingerers we all liked trips to Mildenhall as we had the use of the American Air Force canteen. After a further course I was posted to Ely Hospital on the officers' ward.

"Towards the end of my service in the RAF I was posted to North Wales as one of the medical support team for the unit disposing of German nerve gas bombs. These were very dangerous weapons and we could not afford any mistakes handling them. As it was we had a blood test every week.

"At the age of 21 I completed my three year service in the RAF and was demobbed in Sutton Coldfield. I went to work at different tasks around the village. This included some time at Roys' Nursery at Mill

Green and with Bobbins as an electrician. Then in November 1961 I married Myrtle Hewitt whom I had known for some time, having been introduced to her by my sister. She was married to Myrtle's brother. So brother and sister Shell married brother and sister Hewitt. Myrtle was one of seven children.

"I took a part time job as a gardener at Westgate Hall, then a Norfolk County Council home for the elderly, and I also became a part time carer. When the gardening job was reorganised I became a full time carer there. Myrtle was a care assistant at Cranmer House in Fakenham, but I continued to cycle to and from Westgate Hall. Then we moved on to Sidney Dye House in Kings Lynn which was an old peoples' home – long closed now to make way for a private care home. Myrtle was the assistant matron and we lived in a flat on the site. When we left there we had nowhere to live and moved in with my mother in Church Walk.

"I saw two jobs advertised on the same day. One was with Lady Fermoy at Hillington and the other with the Russell Smiths at Burnham Norton Lodge. I chose the latter and Myrtle and I worked in that big house and garden for the Russell Smiths until they both died within a very short time of each other three years later. Mr Russell Smith was a delightful man with a passion for golf. He liked me to stand by the Vine House at 9 a.m. each day so he could say good morning. He was a stickler for time and if, for some reason, I was not there he would not wait.

"Mrs Russell Smith, Audrey Earle's mother, drove herself around in an electric wheelchair. She had six ancient Jersey cows of which she thought the world. They were beyond milking.

"In 1956 I first met Vice Admiral Sir Hector Maclean who was the magistrate who swore me in as a Special Constable at the start of 31 very happy years of service attached to the Police Force. We had no uniform in the early days – just an armband, a badge, a book of instructions and a notebook. We would come to the fore on election day or at an event which drew crowds. There were two regular police constables in the village at the time, PC Lionel Hewitt and PC Mike Dixon. PC 'Beefy' Snelling had been the constable for years but this was after his time. We established a good working relationship with the PCs and were very useful to them and to new appointees with our local knowledge. When the police became more mobile we would sometimes go out on patrol with them.

"I was attached to the unit at Hunstanton and was promoted to Section Officer (equivalent to Inspector) in 1980, responsible for the 14 or 15 Specials from Peterstone to Dersingham. We held training nights and were allocated our duties by the Norfolk Constabulary from Hunstanton or Kings Lynn according to the scale of the task. We worked closely with the Royal Protection Squad at Sandringham and I was on duty there regularly, including every Christmas Day for many years at the church.

"Special Constables were mainly on foot beat and when in uniform had the same powers and authority as regular police. It was comforting to law abiding citizens to see a Bobby on the beat, keeping our eyes open. In my days as Section Officer at Hunstanton I encouraged female Specials and we had a higher percentage of them than almost anywhere else in the county.

"Among the big occasions were the floods of 1978 which did a lot of damage in the Hunstanton area. Then there were horse trials and the Burnham Flower Show each summer. We also had to investigate reports of missing persons and this could entail some harrowing experiences. We were looking for one missing person and I almost wrecked my car in a ditch before we found him. He had taken some pills but we managed to revive him. Then he hanged himself a week later. And there were moments which are amusing looking back but which caused consternation at the time, such as the undertaker who forgot to apply the handbrake to the hearse parked at the top of a hill. It rolled off on its own as soon as the coffin was loaded.

"As I approached retirement from the Specials – an event I had delayed as long as I could, I received a letter from the Prime Minister awarding me the MBE. The Queen's personal detective rang to say he had compiled some notes about me to brief the Queen for the day itself. His very clear advice was 'if it ain't right don't argue'. The Deans were a great support for the big day. They treated us to London by train, we stayed in a hotel and went to see *Phantom of the Opera* the night before. The next day a chauffeur-driven limousine picked us up and drove us through the crowds and through the gates of the Palace. Mr Dean's Secretary was with us for the Investiture. I was overwhelmed with letters and cards of congratulations – some from people I had not seen for decades, such as the son of the owner of the Dereham nursery where I had worked all those years ago.

"I have been involved with the British Legion since 1957. When I joined I was assured that there was nothing to do except belong and turn out on Remembrance Sunday. However, by 1960 I was branch Treasurer and then Secretary from 1970 when I took over from Donald Hall. He had been a roundsman for Dudley Bower the grocer. I served on the County Committee and became Group President and Chairman. The Burnham Market branch still has 41 members.

"I was at the 80th anniversary parade of the British Legion and being in the front rank was inspected by the Duke of Edinburgh. He stopped and asked me what branch of the service I had been in. When I told him it was the RAF he added 'And the Police' and moved on. I shall never know if he was briefed or whether it was my police medal that gave him the information." Stafford Snell was awarded the Certificate of Appreciation by the British Legion, Eastern Area in 1986 and has two Certificates of Appreciation for his work for the poppy appeal.

"Burnham Norton village used to lie to the north of St Margaret's church in Bellamy's Lane before plague forced it to be abandoned and was resettled about a mile further north on the other side of what is now the coast road. Its earlier settlement was in closer proximity to Friars Lane and there are rumours that a tunnel exists between the Friary ruins and St Margaret's church. Most of Burnham Norton is part of the Holkham Estate. At one time coal boats would moor at its wharf. The land was reclaimed and the marshes drained by the Earl of Orford in the late 1800s and some of the marshes were cultivated for arable production during the war."

As it is, Burnham Norton village ends abruptly at the edge of the marshes, now a haven for sea birds and walkers. The single village pub, The Prince of Wales, closed years ago and is now a private house occupied by the Francis family. Teddy Francis was a clever iron work craftsman for Hill & Osborne. His father was drowned in the *Hood*, sunk by the *Bismark*.

Stafford Snell has been Clerk to the Parish Meeting in Burnham Norton for 15 years and in that time has added the Clerkship of three Parish Councils: South Creake for 10 years, Burnham Market for five when he took over from Neville Steel and Burnham Thorpe for two when Neville Steel sadly died. "I was arm twisted into this work by Bernard Phillips and over the years the rules and regulations have become ever more complicated. Big changes are signalled for Parish

Councillors where a new code of conduct and declaration of interests are demanded. The days when the minute book was the main output of the Clerk's work are gone.

"I was a member of the old agricultural workers' union and secretary of the branch for many years. I used to travel around collecting subs in the Burnhams and Brancaster. This has all been absorbed by the Transport and General Workers Union today. For a time I sat on their Horticultural Advisory Committee which met in London.

"Because of my Special Constable duties I could not get involved in a number of activities which I would have found interesting. I was invited at one time to apply to become a magistrate and I had to resign temporarily from the Specials at the time of my interview – having been assured that if I did not become a magistrate the job was there to be resumed immediately. I went through all the stages and at the last they decided that I might be biased or embarrassed when face to face with one of my former 'clients' and so I returned to uniform within 24 hours."

Burnham Thorpe

Mary Heather

Just after the turn of the 20th century two farming families converged on Burnham Thorpe. In 1901 the Stubbs who were to be Mary Heather's maternal grandparents were dairy farming in Rutland. They had five children with a year between each of them and their father wanted to emigrate to Canada. Their mother had other ideas. Mr Stubbs knew Mr Christie at Creake who told him of a spare farm on the Orford Estate at Burnham Thorpe. So he duly made the journey by train and visited the farm in question – Manor Farm situated near the church. He looked around the farm and concluded it would do. On his return to Rutland his wife asked him about the farm and particularly about the house. But he had to confess that he had concentrated on the farm and had not noticed the house. However, since the farm would support them and their five children he assumed the house would suit them too. So they packed up the farm, house, animals, implements and all their goods and transported them to Burnham Market by special train. They loaded up carts for the final part of the journey to Thorpe.

"My future grandmother saw the Manor House for the first time and agreed it would do very well!" says Mary.

In 1903 the Howards came to live at East End farm which was then also part of the Orford Estate with connections with Lord Walpole who is still Lord of the Manor of Burnham Thorpe. They had started on a small farm at Thursford, and progressed to a larger farm at Massingham and then the Cranmer Home farm before settling at Burnham Thorpe. The Howards were to become the paternal grandparents of Mary Howard /Heather.

Mary Heather with Clydo and Anna

"My grandfather Howard was farmer and coal merchant. His wife died giving birth to their second child. She was Reg Mussett of Gallow Hill's mother and he had to bring in a housekeeper. It was impossible for a farmer to bring up two daughters on his own. In due course he married the housekeeper and they had two children, my father and aunt. They were all brought up as one family.

"Years later my grandmother Howard had the awful experience of the aftermath of an accident which resulted in the death of my grandfather and rendered her son unconscious. They were both brought home from Overy marshes in the bottom of a cart pulled by a carthorse driven by one of the farm workers. My grandfather had a bad heart and he and his son were on the marshes rounding up horses when one bolted and dragged my father to unconsciousness. The shock of seeing this gave grandfather Howard a heart attack from which he died instantly.

"After my grandfather's early demise in 1912, my father took over the running of East End farm where, apart from his service in the Norfolk Yeomanry in the Great War, he farmed until his death in 1962. He married my mother in 1922 uniting Manor and East End farms. My mother was now the eldest of seven Stubbs children and my grandmother Howard moved to live in the Shooting Box.

"It is now the home of Lady Glenconner whilst the Manor House is home to Lady Silvia Combe, a daughter of the former Earl of Leicester. Both these ladies remember and discuss my associations with these two houses and their associated farms. My maternal family lived at Crabbe Hall farm and worked the farm from 1925 to 1934.

"I went to school first to St Monica's in Overy Staithe situated in what is now Dr Wright's house. It was wartime and pupils who passed their 11+ usually went to Fakenham Grammar School. However, in the blackout, cycling to Burnham Market, catching two trains and walking from the LNER station in Fakenham to school, reversing the process in the evening, was too much for my mother to contemplate. So I went instead to board at Dereham High School in the company of Jean and Diana Shearer, the Bower twins and the Bells from Overy. Later I stayed with an uncle and aunt in Dereham.

"I went on to teachers training college at St Gabriels in Camberwell, London and started my teaching career with East End kids who were a pleasure. Then I spent two years in Essex teaching seniors before returning to Fakenham for seven years teaching at the Secondary School. I spent 26 years at the Secondary Modern Smithdon High School in Hunstanton until I retired with a long service award in the late 1980s. I taught PE, maths, English, arts and crafts and with great delight I meet ex pupils regularly in the villages. One of them, Alison Ayres, whose father runs the coal merchants in Stanhoe, trained to be a stone mason and is working in Coventry on the old cathedral. Recently I saw her in Burnham Market for the first time in years and she threw her arms about me in a touching reunion.

"When my father died my mother and I designed and built our present bungalow in Thorpe. She died in 1972. After her death I was told by the doctor that I needed a complete break, whether it was climbing in the Himalayas or touring America. A friend of mine contacted a travel agent and showed me a brochure for the maiden, round the world, voyage of the *QEII*. At first I dismissed this idea of joining such a project. I was teaching and could not give up my job.

"However the idea grew on me and I negotiated a term's leave of absence and set off from Burnham Thorpe with mixed feelings. After all I would be travelling on my own and who would want to speak to me on a smart ship like that? I packed loads of books but as it happened I hardly opened one of them. Not only did I find the experience very friendly and stimulating but I met my future husband, Maurice, who was a steward aboard and had sailed in liners for years. We went on shore trips together and it was the holiday of a lifetime. We were married in 1981. This brought me the joy of three step sons. So although I married late I had an instant family. Maurice died from lung cancer in 1995."

Mary Heather is a pillar of the community. She was awarded the Unsung Heroes certificate by the Mayor of Kings Lynn in 2000 for her selfless work for others in the community. She was the organist at Overy Church every Sunday for 16 years and played as second organist as required at Burnham Thorpe – especially on the big occasions. For the last 30 years she has been organist at All Saints. "I took music lessons from the age of seven and started on the piano. However, I was introduced to the organ and had lessons and played for services in the college chapel. I had lessons on the Southwark Cathedral organ during my time in London.

"Like my parents and grandparents before me I am a church warden. My four grandparents, two aunts, two uncles and husband lie in the churchyard. My grandparents took on this role soon after the church had been restored to celebrate Nelson's memory and it was deeply in debt as a result. They helped to clear the debt with fund raising activity. My activities were temporarily interrupted by a rare form of tumour on the nerve leading from the ear to the brain. They diagnosed it in time but it still needed five and a half hours of surgery to remove it. It has left me deaf in one ear but I was restored to full activity in a remarkably short time." Mary explains, "I had to get back to my dogs.

"I am joint chairperson of the Nelson Memorial Hall and Secretary of the Buntings charity. Richard Bunting born in 1601 was a rich merchant and ship owner. He decided to set up a charity to educate the children of Burnham Thorpe and set aside £12 per annum for this purpose. This paid for a school-master to give lessons in 'the chamber of the malthouse in Burnham Thorpe'. However, after Richard Bunting died in 1680 his widow and heirs allowed these payments to lapse and the default was investigated in a court case in 1784 when the then owner of the 'manor' was ordered to pay the arrears for the missing 104 years. Hence a properly endowed school came into existence and 11 trustees were appointed.

"These included Horatio Lord Walpole, the Hon. Horatio Walpole, the Earl of Orford and the Revd Edmund Nelson, Rector of Burnham Thorpe. The result was the establishment of a more substantial building with a full time schoolmaster. The accounts for the period 1829 to 1833 showed that the schoolmaster, Mr Erasmus Greenwood, was paid a salary of £12. 13 shillings and 3 pence per half year and he did not get an increase during that time. In 1966 the local education authority ceased to maintain the school and closure followed. The Charity Commissioners directed that the money be invested in an official charity fund and the Richard Bunting Educational Fund was set up. It is for the benefit of children who reside in the village to apply for help with, for example, school uniform. The nursery rhyme Baby Baby Bunting is supposed to be connected with this benefactor.

"I remember the celebrations for the Coronation of 1953. The Parish Council meeting to plan it for the village was held at East End farm.

"There was a house to house collection to raise funds and a New Year Social and Dance. Every child under 15 was to have a Coronation mug with sweets. Men over 65 would be presented with 1oz of tobacco and women over 65 with half a lb of tea in a Coronation canister. A seat was erected, trees planted and tea provided for children and old age pensioners. A highlight on the day itself was the first television set ever in the village, hired from Uttings by Mary's grandfather and set up in the Nelson Hall. All the farms entered decorated floats for the celebrations and I can remember being dressed as Britannia, sitting on top of our float from East End farm.

"There is a visitors book in the Church which attracts large numbers of claimed relationships with Nelson as well as descendants of tradesmen who purport to have supplied his hats and other possessions. It would be impossible for any man to have owned so much or had so many relatives. However, one of the few remaining people, at the time, who had connections directly with Nelson, was Mrs Valiant High living in North Creake in 1900.

"She had married the grandson of Nelson's nurse and often heard her father describe the sayings and doings of the Hero of Trafalgar. This man, Valiant, won the Admiral's favour at a dinner Nelson gave for the village at the Nelson Inn at Burnham Thorpe before he took command of the *Agamemnon* in 1793. He was a lad at the time and thought he should have been invited to the feast. He was loud in his complaint to his friends but was greeted by derision. He went for the chief offender – a youth double his size– and fought him tooth and nail. Nelson witnessed this scrap and declared that it was a 'right valiant fight'. From then on the youth was known as Valiant. He wanted to go to sea with Nelson but had to wait until 1801 when he took part in the Battle of Copenhagen. In 1876 as an old man he was invited to the Rectory in Burnham Thorpe by the Revd Levien. Valiant gave the rector a small scrubbing brush from his ship at the Battle of Copenhagen and this was passed down the Levien family. The name Valiant was carried down to the original Valiant's son."

Whilst the spirit of Nelson and pride in its hero is all about in the village, it has nonetheless managed to avoid vulgar commercialism and exploitation of the nation's greatest sailor. As Mary Heather recalls, "A huge black limousine with blackened windows was crawling around the village when it stopped opposite me and its windows were wound down to reveal two middle aged couples in their Sunday suits. They started berating me that there were no brown tourist signs to help visitors find a Nelson Centre, and how this was all behind the times. I let them finish and then said that they would not have been able to stop their car and talk to a villager who had lived here all her life if commercialism had been developed, and told them the locals preferred their unspoilt village. To their credit they saw the point and laughed, wound up their blackened windows and drove off to explore for themselves.

"When the village celebrates Nelson we do it with duty to history rather than tourists in mind. The 150th anniversary of Trafalgar in 1955 is an example. On a stormy Norfolk October day a great gathering assembled representing all aspects of local life plus those who had moved away from their roots in Burnham Thorpe and returned for the reunion. The Bishop of Norwich conducted the service, then, led by the band of the Royal Marines, we processed out of the church through the windswept graves to the reception in the Nelson Hall. Captain Maclean from the Admiralty then spoke of Nelson the professional sailor. My father was Chairman of the Parish council at the time. We had an extensive exhibition of pictures and memorabilia in the Hall for the occasion and some of the Thorpers had been at the Centenary celebrations 50 years before.

"I was a Parish Councillor for many years but came to the conclusion that its powers were so limited that I could better spend my time for the good of the village doing other things. Many of these are related to the church where my family has been actively involved for three generations. There is usually a fund raising event to collect for, which keeps me running about the village. I went to adult learning college to master my computer and I can now produce bill posters and other publicity for village events. I also sell poppies in October/November. Burnham Thorpe has retained its integrity as a proper village and it is interesting how many Thorpers and their families come back to the village to take part in its activities even though they live elsewhere."

Amongst Mary Heather's many talents is her painting. "I paint in gouache which is somewhere between oils and watercolours. I find oils too messy and they tend to get everywhere. The use of pastel gives a certain texture and it can be effective on its own or with gouache. Recently I have changed to watercolours. I have exhibited paintings for years and still manage to sell a few each year." But her pride and joy are her two West Highland terriers, Clydo and Anna. Originally they were bred to keep the cats down in the Highlands of Scotland. They will see off any cat who dares to come near the house – except one. This has one black eye and is called Nelson.

The house where she was born

Tom Mahon

Tom Mahon was born in the Lord Nelson pub in Burnham Thorpe where his mother was the landlady. She was born Lucy Johnson and her father was steward at Ivy Farm. Her mother came from Wells.

"My father to be was born in Sheffield and was descended from Irish stock as his family name would imply, the Mc having been dropped at some distant point in the past. He served in the First World War but was injured in the knee and, on being invalided out, was sent to help the war effort on a farm. This was his introduction to Burnham Thorpe and to Lucy Johnson whom he later married. He worked at Ivy Farm, at the time tenanted from the Leicester Estates by Mr Ringer. I was born in 1929, one of two sons and two daughters, one of whom is still living in Burnham Thorpe.

"I attended Burnham Thorpe school which at the time was still funded by the Richard Bunting Trust. As we did in those days, I left at the age of

Tom Mahon

14 and went to work at Ivy Farm. Whilst still at school I had been through the sequence of elevator boy, holgee boy and rake boy over the successive harvest times. My wages when I started full time work were 24/6d per week. I soon moved from Ivy Farm to Manor Farm which was by this time tenanted from the Leicester Estate by Mr Youngs. Manor Farm is now Leith House Farm.

"I was promoted to standing loader, still at 24/6d per week and over the two weeks of harvest we tried to make this £5 by long hours and continual hard work. Later Manor Farm became vacant and the tenancy was taken over by Garry Maufe for whom I worked for 50 years, firstly as tractor driver and for the last 10 years as foreman."

This record of loyal service was deserving of recognition. Tom Mahon continued, "When I started at the 500 acre Manor Farm on 25th September 1945 at the age of 14 there were 18 hands employed there in addition to myself. When I left after 50 years service there were just two of us and I was given a barometer.

"We grew sugar beet, barley, wheat, and peas. The Manor House had been empty for a long while but then Lady Sylvia Combe, sister of Lord Leicester, and her husband Major Simon Combe, moved in. Lady Sylvia lives there still. We acquired some new malting barley seed, enough for five acres, and it lay in sacks in the barn. Major Combe, who was a director of Watney Combe and Reid, and the leading influence in defeating an unwelcome takeover bid, came to look at the seed. He took it in his hands and said he would buy from us all we could grow.

"I was involved in planning, planting and managing the 14 acres of plum orchard at Leith House since its beginnings over 20 years ago. Plum trees reach their peak in about 25 years so there is a continual programme of renewal to ensure continuity. We also grew two acres of apples in that orchard and every year employed a gang of women to pick the fruit, pack it and send it to London and other markets. The development of pick it yourself has reduced the picking gang and my family organised it for many years."

Tom Mahon recalled some of his early days in Burnham Thorpe. "I had a gang of friends who shared my delight in mild mischief. We must have been a real pain in the butt when we were seven or eight. If there was snow on the ground we would make snow balls and try to lob them into chimneys to put the fire out. There was one shop in Burnham Thorpe – run by Fred Huggins. This was combined post office, general store and blacksmith. He always seemed to us kids to be a difficult old man. Perhaps that is not surprising when I think of the way we played him up.

"The blacksmith was Bob Robinson and we would go into the blacksmith's shop with a horseshoe we had found. That would be worth four sweets in the shop. That same horseshoe was found more than once. We would also kick Mr Huggins' door when it had just been painted and this must have irritated him with good reason. There was Algar and Curry, carpenters and wheelwrights, run by two brothers. The big logs were hand sawed over a pit by two people with a 'push me / pull you' saw, one in the pit and one above. We made a hole in the bottom of the pit allowing the river Burn to flood it and then we would play pirates in the flood waters. I was trying to walk the plank in hobnailed boots and fell in. The pit dried out when the river Burn ceased to flow which it did each summer. This continued until the river was deepened in the 1950s.

"I was 10 years old in 1939. We had 10 weeks of snow that year and each of us searched for suitable wood to make a sledge as this was the only way of getting around. The school was closed for a while through a combined epidemic of mumps, German measles and chicken pox. I can remember the Blenheim bomber coming down at Gravel Pit Hill in Thorpe. Also, later on when I was driving a tractor, I recall using it as cover from machine gun bullets from a German plane which was trying to unload its ammunition, having lost its way and being chased by the RAF. I can see the bullets now, spitting through the grass, and can hear them clanging against the tractor. There was the radar station on top of Beacon Hill and searchlight units on the Ringstead road and at Lodge Hill, Burnham Thorpe. There were also numerous airfields in the area so we were a target for enemy bombing.

"One of the bakers who served Thorpe in those days was George Trett from Burnham Market. He made wonderful bread. My wife Audrey worked for him and did another round each day in the Overy, Brancaster area." Audrey's father who was a Hubbard, was born in Overy. He was one of seven children, three girls and four boys.

He moved from Overy first to Fring and then to Anmer. When Audrey was three years old the family moved to Field Barn, Burnham Market.

"George's pony knew the round and the routine. The first stop was the Lord Nelson pub where, by arrangement, George would have a pint of beer often serving himself in the cellar where he left the money for it.

"There was no policeman in Burnham Thorpe although PC Snelling from Burnham Market and his assistants Don Long and Tom Buckland would keep an eye on the place from time to time.

"The winter of 1947 was bitter with heavy snow fall. We spent much of our time snow heaving and had permission to take the tractor and trailer over the fields to bring essential supplies to the village. George Moorhouse and Jack Grint were rival coal merchants in Burnham Market and supplied coal with instructions that their coal should only be delivered to their own customers. Of course we did not know who they were and in the emergency it did not seem to matter. All the coal looked the same and was the same price. Presumably George and Jack collected the money later from their customers, irrespective of whose coal they had received. George Moorhouse was a big man who lived on Chalk Hill and seemed to us to be half a hermit.

"During meat rationing one of the butchers in Burnham Market, long since departed the scene, is reputed to have stretched the meat available by picking up a dead sheep from the marshes which had died from 'shortage of breath'. He would drive it back in his van making 'baa baa' noises to make believe it was still alive and then offer it as a bit of extra mutton to his hard pressed customers. No one starved in the Burnhams during rationing. Poverty was always a serious challenge and the larger families would have to use every bit of food. This would include for example, picking the meat out of the neck and head of a pheasant to make it go round for the family.

"Audrey and I were married in 1952. We lived for a while in the Peterstone brick yard. We had met at one of the old fashioned dances where Mr Starling, the AA man, taught us all to dance. He was big of girth but very light on his feet. There was a dance in one village hall or another three nights a week. We have six children, two boys and four girls. Our son David runs the landscape gardening business with which I help him, and one of our daughters is a school teacher in Crete. Another is a nurse. We have 11 grandchildren and one died, sadly, of meningitis.

"For many years I have been involved with the Burnham Market Horticultural Society. It has been going for more than 100 years and has a long association with the Carnival which was the centre of the village's annual activities for so long. I started my association 45 years ago when the ever persuasive Reggie Baldry was its chairman. He was also the village postman and got around to everyone in the village. He asked me to come and give him a hand on the gate and I was pleased to get involved for the sake of the children whose participation in the show was never very strong.

"I was invited onto the committee and gave up being chairman after a number of years. However, the fortunes of the Society were going down and down and I was invited to come back and raise it up again. It is not easy. People do not have the gardens or the interest they had years ago and it is a struggle to get younger people interested. It would be a great pity to see it fold up and we are trying hard to give it renewed life."

Burnham Overy

Bernard Phillips

Sidney and Mary Theresa Phillips, Bernard's paternal grandparents, ran a distillery business in London with Sidney's brother until they fell out with him. They holidayed in Burnham Overy in one of the beach huts on Scolt Head Island which was described in a brochure as a 'Romantic North Sea Island'. They were met at Burnham Market station by Alan Bell the local taxi driver and motor engineer and introduced to Billy Haines who, with his rivals Laddie Lane and Welcome Thompson, catered for the needs of the occupants of the beach huts, supplying groceries, household equipment and water. These huts, with primitive sanitation and running water, were a hazard to health.

Bernard explains, "Sidney and Mary Theresa had seven children: three girls and four boys. One of these was George, my father. His younger brother William was a doctor at Kings Lynn hospital but was drowned on *HMS Niger* off Iceland during the war. The children were teenagers by the time the family came on holiday to Burnham Overy. They fell in love with the place. My grandfather was eccentric. He got married and had children but his parents were unaware of this even though they lived close by.

"On holiday, the family used to shop in Burnham Market where they drifted into the Hoste Arms where an auction was in progress. For sale, in several lots, was

Bernard Phillips

the big estate in Overy of Sir Henry Webb. My grandparents bought two lots which included Staithe House, some derelict barns and maltings, all very cheap and all on impulse. They had not seen the property and seem to have been unaware there was a sitting tenant (a famous actress) in Staithe House. It took them five years to gain vacant possession. In the meantime, with the help of Fisher Haines, Billy's brother, they made the Well House on the main road habitable and moved into it.

"My father's elder sister, my aunt Mary, ran an hotel in Sutton, Surrey. She thought the property in Burnham Overy would make a marvellous hotel. Her parents agreed and began renovating it for that purpose, starting with the maltings. In the late 1920s they gained possession of Staithe House – that is the original house of that name and not St Monica's school whose name was later changed to Staithe House. During this work my grandfather spent most of his time running a motor boat called 'The Dorothy' leaving my grandmother and her daughters to help. The finished hotel had 30 bedrooms.

"My father, George, went to sea as one of the cadets from *HMS Conway,* the training ship made famous in John Masefield's books. Later he joined the Elders and Fyffes banana boats and, while on leave in Dulwich, met the girl who was to become my mother. She was not a Catholic and my grandparents insisted that she entered the faith before she married their son. Grandmother Phillips smoked and read a lot, was very Irish and a paid up member of Sinn Fein. My future mother was baptised a Catholic just before the wedding in 1935.

"They moved to The Moorings but it was not a happy welcome for my mother. She was vivacious and attractive and a qualified administrator who had been happily working for the Institute of Gas Engineers in London. She was swallowed up by the stodgy, if eccentric, Phillips family who neither understood nor appreciated her freshness and innocence. She was devoted to my father but was very unhappy, employed for nothing to work in the hotel.

"I was born in 1937 in The Moorings, delivered by Dr Hicks from Wells, in room number 16 where my grandfather died four years later. There were complications at the birth and my sister who was born in 1939 was delivered in Dulwich. One of my godfathers was Andrew Butler, the distinguished architect who eventually wrote a three volume biography of Lutyens. Although known as Andrew, his first name was, in fact, Arthur. He lived in Gong Lane, Overy Staithe, with his sister and mother. His father was the son of the Victorian feminist Josephine Butler.

"The war started slowly and it was not until 1940 that the hotel was requisitioned by the War Office. The family were allowed to keep the old maltings whilst Staithe House and grounds were taken over for the duration. The furniture was stored in the old maltings end. With the men gone to war, Mother was there alone with three children in squalid conditions. She needed all her considerable strength and resilience to survive. Grandmother had left for Mary's hotel in Sutton but came up to The Moorings from time to time. Mother raised food to help out the London relatives; the LNER provided a reliable link.

"The hotel had been registered as a limited company in the 1930s and after my grandfather's death my grandmother owned all 100 shares. This was not significant at the time. My grandfather had died in 1941 and there was negligible compensation to come from the depredations of the war which had all but destroyed the fabric of the hotel. So in 1945 my grandmother, rather than face the enormous challenge of rebuilding it all again, put it on the market.

"At the auction at the Hoste Arms it failed to reach its £1000 reserve and my grandmother offered to place it with my parents if they thought they could make a go of it. My father had left the Royal Navy, following his war service in Combined Operations at Dieppe, Sicily and Normandy. He won the DSC and was mentioned in despatches with a personal commendation from Mountbatten. He had some experience in helping run the hotel in the 1930s when he left the sea and helped in the kitchen. So they took the hotel on, tidied up the maltings and opened for business for the summer of 1946. By 1948 they had extended it to the whole building. Many of its 30 rooms were booked from summer to summer by regulars who remained loyal despite the closure in war years. Professor Solly and Joan Zuckerman always had room 14, for example. My parents were helped to get it all up and running by Nelson Scoles who lived in Gong Lane in 'Stokers'.

"Overy attracted many people from Cambridge who loved to watch birds, sail and play golf at Brancaster. Blakeney had done so for many years before but as Overy was discovered it attracted its own loyal clientele. Many years later one of the highlights was the reunion of John Cockcroft, the father of the British atom bomb, and his opposite number, Peter Kapitza from Russia, brought together by Solly Zuckerman. Many of our clients later found houses in the area. The Zuckermans bought and upgraded a fine house in Burnham Thorpe using Jack Bickell's firm as the builder, until they parted company. Later Lord Zuckerman was attended by a security team whenever he came to Thorpe, reflecting the secret and sensitive nature of his work as Scientific Adviser to successive Prime Ministers. His widow Joan, a talented artist, outlived him for many years and she was a kind and generous person. She was the daughter of the Marquis of Reading and in her widowhood resumed her Jewish observance.

"Many war wives became war widows and Burnham Overy was a sad place in the mid 1940s. Sir Matthew Smith and his wife Gwen lost two sons in the war. There were many others who grieved.

"We were not allowed on the beach during the war. Technically this was an invasion coast and there were numerous gun batteries stationed behind Overy. They would practise by shooting over our heads at targets on Scolt Head or out at sea. This completed the destruction of most of the beach huts which were never replaced after the war. Nonetheless Addy Outred, who helped Mother with the pigs and the ducks, would come in with bullets and other armaments he had found. We would help him extract the cordite and make fireworks which we would explode in The Moorings garden. There were also some hollow trees opposite and we found detonators in them – at least that is what we thought they were with their porcelain and wires. We also found a cache of ammunition in the bank of the small mill stream over the Carnser. Our pranks were reported to the police and one day we looked up to find PC Snelling watching us. Addy died while on holiday in Turkey in 2001. His initials remain, carved on a beech tree in Staithe House garden.

"Another resident of Overy was the engraver Robert Austin who lived in the Chapel at the end of the Bank. He was responsible for our bank note, coin and stamp designs. There were a number of formidable ladies, one of whom once saw someone maltreating a young child on the beach. She intervened saying this was no way to treat a child and she would adopt her, which she did.

"My mother had served in the WRVS who were responsible for the evacuees of whom there were many from London. The War Office prepared plans to evacuate everyone in the event of an invasion but said they should be kept secret to avoid spreading alarm. The logic of evacuating Londoners to a potential invasion coast defeated the local ladies in charge. Anyway the news got out and the evacuees drifted home. The ladies of the WRVS were in trouble as a result, with accusations of violating the Official Secrets Act directed at them, but the evacuees had a rotten time, branded as they were as second class citizens. A few stayed on.

"I went to school at St Monica's. It was run at the time by two 'brown' nuns: Sister Mable Grace who was the daughter of Samual Palmer a previous owner of the maltings and Staithe House, and Miss Ridewood. They were later assisted by Mrs Hattersley, the widow of a distinguished army doctor. Then the school was sold to the Trengroves. One of their daughters became the artist Pamela Noyes. She was married to Murray Noyes whose parents lived in Coastguard Cottages. She is still one of the more successful artists but others struggled and one paid the coal bills with pictures!

"When I left St Monica's I went to St Edmund's, the Roman Catholic School near Ware in Hertfordshire. I won a scholarship to read English at Emmanuel College Cambridge, where I met with many a Moorings devotee (town and gown) and was often entertained by them. In 1962 I was in France where I met and married Carla who is an American from the Bronx. Her grandparents came to America as Jewish immigrants from Russia. Carla is an accomplished artist, notably drawing and etching. Her father became a distinguished engineer and cardiologist: he invented the Pacemaker.

"In 1965 my father was taken ill. He had never been fully fit since D Day in 1944. We came back to help run the hotel. With the change in the table licence laws the hotel started making money and became very successful. However, family storms were gathering. My grandmother had died in 1952 and she had distributed her 100 shares, worthless at the time, among members of the family.

"By the early 1960s this distribution became very significant. My father and mother, who did all the work and were responsible for the growing success of the business, found themselves with 49% of the shares. Whilst two of his siblings, who were seldom there, had 51%. However, even though they had a majority of the shares they were in a minority on the Board of Directors and did not seem to realise that to correct this position and reflect their majority shareholding they would have to sack one or two directors. They thought they could do more with the capital than with the not inconsiderable dividends they were already receiving.

"I decided to raise the funds to buy the company and meet the valuation of £45,000. I had been encouraged over the years by loyal clients offering their financial help if ever I decided to buy out the company. I raised some small amounts of £200 or £300. Then an old customer who lived in Burnham Norton and who loved The Moorings, phoned to say he would be prepared to give 20. I thanked him saying that £20 would not take us very far, only to discover that he meant £20,000! I made the offer which was accepted by the old-look Board of Directors.

"Eventually my uncle Gerald and aunt Grace, the shareholders, were advised by their lawyer to restructure the Board to reflect their majority. They withdrew the acceptance and we were all flung out. This was at the end of October 1969. The hotel had an 85% occupancy rate during its months of opening in the summer – well above the national average. We were fully booked for the following summer. The logistics of the hotel made a separation of our house from the hotel impractical: the hotel kitchen was joined to our house but the new owners decided to bar us entry to the hotel.

"We returned from Sunday Mass to find that Uncle Gerald had sealed the door with six-inch screws. Much of the furniture in the hotel was ours and we were determined to get it back. So I replaced the six-inch screws with half-inch ones and while it did not look as if there was any difference I could open the door at will. A final deal had not yet been signed and I refused to hand over the keys of the wine cellar until it was. However, my uncle managed to break down the cellar door and drank himself to death. He died the following March, estranged from his wife and living in the opposite end of their house in Essex.

"It was all a disaster. The executors of his will insisted that a professional manager be appointed. Geoff Goff from the Jolly Sailors at Brancaster came for a year and did a very competent job. However, having put the hotel back on its feet he was sacked. The last straw was the introduction of VAT in the early 1970s. The whole sorry tale broke my father's heart and he died the following year.

"The hotel was sold to Gervase Steele. He did up the Georgian end and sliced up the rest like a pie into seven or eight dwellings. He kept the lawn to the water's edge and the owners benefited from this amenity.

"I decided to do something completely different so became a teacher. I taught for 14 years, until 1986, at King Edward VII School in Kings Lynn where I became head of the English department. We lived at Rest Harrow in Friars Lane, Burnham Norton.

"Carla and I had started a monthly publication which we called *The Paper*, a North Norfolk magazine, full of interesting features from different contributors although at first we wrote much of it ourselves! We were looking for a food columnist and Carla agreed to write it under the pseudonym 'Cocote'. The *Sunday Times* was running a 'Best Cook' competition and Carla entered one of her recipes. To our surprise and delight, it made the quarter finals and then won the final."

Bernard and Carla

Carla takes up the story. "The competition was sponsored by British Gas and the prize was a state of the art gas cooker. This seemed to be a strange prize as there was no gas in Burnham Norton and the sponsors were somewhat miffed to see me posing in the *Sunday Times* with my winning entry with our wood burning stove in the background.

"Doubtless the expectation was for a Hampstead or modern Burnham Market type to win and we have not seen a similar competition in the *Sunday Times* since. Nonetheless the feature drew attention from interested readers, some of whom placed catering orders with us to be supplied from home.

"The following summer Justin de Blank and Lord Coke opened a restaurant at the tea rooms in the Ancient House in Holkham village and asked me to cook on two or three nights a week. The other nights were allocated elsewhere and the variation in quality from one night to another screwed up the image for all of us. It was not the way to run a restaurant and I longed for one of my own."

Bernard continued . "There was an ideal location in Wells for the sort of restaurant we had in mind. It was operating as a café and we knew we could do a whole lot better than that. From time to time we would look in and put it to the owner that if he ever decided to sell we would be interested in buying. We had almost given up hope in the face of his continued rejection, when we received a phone call in January 1986 from our accountant that the premises were up for sale at £30,000. Various friends who had promised financial support now failed to come through. Nor were the banks interested in two fifty-year-olds indulging a middle class dream.

"For some years Carla and I had been supporters of the Campaign for Nuclear Disarmament. We could see the sense in being prepared militarily for conflicts as they arose – and most of them were small scale – but we could see no logic or call for nuclear weapons. While visiting London for a National CND meeting, we stayed with Clement Freud's daughter Nicky and John Laflin. When the Wells café came on the market, Nicky and John offered to buy it and renovate it as a restaurant. Two years later we were able to repay them in full. By then the banks *were* interested.

"We ran the Moorings Restaurant for 12 years. It had 35 covers and we opened for lunch four days a week and for dinner five nights a week. This included Sundays and Mondays which were our best days because other places were shut. Our clientele included the owners and staff of other restaurants who were not working those days. As far as possible we served only local organic products. We bought from local fishermen, gardeners and gatherers of wild mushrooms who would appear each day to offer what was available. It was however a great strain and I became ill, so we sold out in July 1998.

"Carla has written half a cookery book and is inspired to finish it. It follows several other successful publications such as *Crabs from the Quayside* and the Norfolk Lavender book of recipes. We also still make the spiced nuts which we served as nibbles in the Moorings."

Bernard and Carla have four children and six grandchildren and still live in Wells. Their influence and encouragement to other restaurateurs in North Norfolk should not be underestimated: they have done much to raise the reputation of the area as a good food destination.

Audrey Earle

Audrey Earle's book *The Boathouse – the Story of a Granary* is a delightful history of this central feature of Burnham Overy Staithe and traces its fortunes from 1824. The granary was a central part of the life of this small village and port during its century as a thriving coastal port. This continued until the channel silted up in the early 20th century and the last small cargo of coal was unloaded in 1923 for Sidney Everitt who was in occupation of the granary at the time.

The building fell into disrepair once its commercial purpose was ended and it was converted into a comfortable family house for holidays with a private anchorage in 1924, reflecting the change in the role of the village. Audrey Earle's study reveals a deep and sensitive attachment to Burnham Overy Staithe and to the characters who made the village. For those interested in this gem of the North Norfolk coast Audrey Earle's book – out of print *pro tem* – is compelling reading.

There were well known families in Overy Staithe. The Phillips family converted the maltster's old house into The Moorings Hotel and this did much to establish Overy Staithe as a popular holiday centre for sailing from the Quay and for golf at Brancaster. Its clientele returned year on year but eventually dwindled as the attractions of the surrounding area encouraged one

Burnham Overy Staithe

after the other to buy or rent a house for themselves. Bernard Phillips owned the successful Moorings restaurant in Wells until the turn of the 21st century.

Audrey Earle describes the evolution of Overy Staithe. "As the character of the Quay changed the Granary became a boathouse and this was inspired by the return to Overy of Billy Haines and his family. Billy had served in the Merchant Navy and the London Fire Brigade before returning to the village of his birth and settling down for the rest of his life. The three Haines brothers, Charlie, Billy and Fisher, married three Tompkin sisters and all the brothers died within a year of each other in 1952–3. Billy and Fisher Haines were joined by George Cleaver at the Quay and for many years helped a succession of holiday makers and leisure sailors to enjoy or improve their sailing skills.

"There were three families, the Haines, the Lanes and the Thompsons, who supplied the milk, newspapers and other essentials by boat from the village to the beach huts on the East Point sand dunes under Gun Hill. At one time there were more than 100 of these beach huts all requiring permission from the Holkham Estate before they could be erected. For many in the area holidaying in a beach hut at Overy was the limit of their purse. The visitors continued to increase each year and Billy Haines ran a passenger boat called *The Rosemary* to the beach.

"The annual Regatta was a popular event with keen local competition in rowing and sailing races. Billy Haines was an immensely popular figure on the Quay with his sturdy figure and rather rolling gait. He had a charming manner, kingfisher blue eyes and a tanned weatherbeaten face, usually wreathed in a smile. He inspired confidence in all attempting the skills of sailing, and his pungent advice to the owners of recalcitrant engines to 'undo everything you can and blow through it …..' was usually successful.

"Billy and Anne Haines lived at Flagstaff House from 1946. A previous owner had been Captain Woodget, Master of the famous clipper *Cutty Sark*.

"By 1960 Peter Beck was the worthy successor to Billy Haines as the driving force behind the Boathouse Company and so he remained for nearly 40 years. Peter was born and bred in Burnham Market but drawn to Overy from an early age by the excitement of small boats and those who sailed them. In 1959 he married Melba Cooper of the well known Wells fishing and lifeboat family and they lived overlooking the Quay for four decades. Peter Beck retired in 2000 and moved into the house originally owned by his father on Overy Road near the end of Friars Lane in Burnham Market.

"William Scoles was a contemporary of Billy Haines and a member of another famous Overy family. The two of them were returning from one of their frequent musseling trips across the Wash in December 1950 in the dark and a blizzard when they went to the assistance of a blazing yacht with four people on board. Three of them were rescued, nearly dead with cold, but the fourth, to the great distress of their rescuers was lost in the icy waters. Billy was awarded a Vellum by the RNLI for his gallantry but he never recovered from his distress. After falling ill with heart trouble he died in 1952 at the age of 62."

Audrey Earle, one of the first Directors of the Boathouse Company from its inauguration in 1959 under the Chairmanship of Elizabeth Cory-Wright, was first introduced to the charm and peace of Overy Staithe in 1936 when her parents took the family there on holiday. She later rented a house at Overy and lived there until she moved in 1953 to Arnolds in Joan Shorts Lane, Burnham Market. This former Wesleyan Chapel had been bought in 1927 by Mrs Arnold for a price, it is thought, of £50 and on which approximately £500 was spent converting it into a private house.

Audrey Earle tells of the sudden appearance of Miss Julia Cook at the gate of Arnolds, "On the day after I moved in this tiny lady in a huge hat appeared at the gate and pointed to the lilies of the valley growing in front of the house. 'You are not to dig those up,' she commanded. 'They were planted by Mrs Arnold and there they are to stay.'" Audrey Earle, who is not easily intimidated by anyone, was nonetheless so taken aback that she agreed to this imperious instruction and there they are to this day.

"I went to art school before the war and have painted in oils and water colours over the years. The life of the area was interrupted by war preparations all around us on the North Norfolk coast. This was designated a potential invasion coast and it was impossible to reach the beach. Holkham beach was the training ground for the Guards Armoured Division in preparation for their landing in Normandy on D Day. I drove an ambulance in Belgium as the Allies pushed forward, evacuating the wounded. Later I was commissioned and posted to France where we distributed Red Cross parcels to released prisoners of war. Then we moved to Brittany. It was a severe winter and driving an ambulance with canvas sides was extremely cold.

"My connections with Overy have been continuous ever since. I had a crab boat for many years, preferring an engine to sail. But the village has been a central part of my life for more than 60 years.

"It is important to encourage the young people of the Burnhams to stay and develop their careers here. I have a cottage in Burnham Market which I let only to local people to get them started in housing which otherwise would be well out of reach in view of the influx of second homers and affluent incomers. I would like to have seen the principle applied in Guernsey adopted in the Burnhams years ago.

"Estate agents in Guernsey have their properties divided into two categories – those reserved for Guernsey residents and those available for incomers. This encourages young people to stay and work on the island in affordable housing, while the properties in price brackets out of their reach are bought by visitors, incomers and second homers who bring wealth and new life to the island. There was potential in the Burnhams to achieve this years ago but the villages have been overwhelmed by empty second homes for 10 months of the year and a huge influx of visitors and holiday makers for two months.

"This puts pressure on shops and services in season and makes it difficult for the shops out of season. The character of the villages has changed as a result and not always for the best. Some of the visitors are inclined to barge about blocking the roads in their 4x4s and jumping the queues in the shops with rude behaviour. I can remember one occasion when a visitor remarked that he found the peasants remarkably pleasant. I touched my forelock and said 'thankee zur'."

One former tenant of Audrey Earle's cottage was David Lingwood. "This really helped me to get started," he says. "I and others are grateful to Miss Earle. She is a very nice lady and I wish there were more like her. She really has the village at heart."

Audrey Earle continues, "The employment base of the district changed radically in the 1950s and 1960s. Where there was a preponderance of farms employing 20 or more people, those same farms can now be worked with one or two. Building and services supporting the growth of second homes have partly replaced the opportunities for the labour market. However, the transition from one structure to the other was a painful experience in the 1960s when the railway went and the villages were in danger of dying. One of the first signals of a new start for the Burnhams was Fitzgeralds delicatessen shop in Burnham Market which attracted a new clientele who went on to make it a desirable and fashionable centre for the well to do.

"I was among the first to have a telephone in the village. It was an amenity that we shared and I would make or receive calls for my neighbours. Despite the changes, the North Norfolk coast and its charming villages remain a unique part of England."